Advance Praise for *It's Debatable*

"In this book, Robert Jensen explores some of the thorniest, most contentious political controversies of our time. Unafraid of fire from the left or the right (and in his life he has experienced both), he boldly takes on hot-button issues that too many of us find ways of sidestepping. Whether you agree with him or not—and I usually do—you will always find a mind thoughtfully exploring, weighing arguments judiciously, and telling you what he thinks, whether it accords with current intellectual fashions or not."
—**Adam Hochschild, University of California Berkeley Graduate School of Journalism, author of *American Midnight: The Great War, a Violent Peace, and Democracy's Forgotten Crisis***

"There is an old Sanskrit verse that says 'Na bruyat satyam apriyam,' which loosely translates to 'don't speak the truth that is unpleasant.' Robert Jensen offers a different approach, reckoning with truths, pleasant and unpleasant, and the disagreements that they generate."
—**M.V. Ramana, School of Public Policy and Global Affairs, University of British Columbia, Vancouver, author of *Nuclear is Not the Solution: The Folly of Atomic Power in the Age of Climate Change***

"It doesn't matter if you agree with Robert Jensen. What matters is that he always, without fail, works to keep us honest. *It's Debatable* takes on the sacred cows of contemporary social justice debates and picks them apart, definition by definition ... Well-sourced, carefully written, compassionate but dogged in its quest for an honest conversation, *It's Debatable* challenges its readers to question their assumptions—every one of them."
—**Mary Angela Bock, School of Journalism and Media, University of Texas at Austin, author of *Seeing Justice: Witnessing, Crime and Punishment in Visual Media***

"Robert Jensen insists he has a mediocre mind, but it's his only false claim in this new book. In actual fact, he's an unconventional critical-thinker and truth-seeker who's unafraid to offend both his foes on the right and his putative allies on the left as he waltzes through minefields to confront some of the most explosive issues of our anxious era."
—**Glenn Frankel, Pulitzer Prize-winning journalist and author of *Shooting Midnight Cowboy: Art, Sex, Loneliness, Liberation, and the Making of a Dark Classic***

"In an age of polarization and groupthink, Robert Jensen has written a how-to manual for independent reasoning that leaves no orthodoxy unscathed. Challenging all political herds, including his own on the left, Jensen situates the gambit of contemporary controversies ... in a clear analysis of white supremacy, patriarchy, and other oppressive hierarchies. His robust treatment of 'wokeness' and 'cancel culture' draws on decades of experience teaching freedom of speech and media law ... An invaluable guide for where we are, how we got here, and what lies ahead."
—**Jason Brownlee, Department of Government, University of Texas at Austin, author of** *Authoritarianism in an Age of Democratization*

"William James defined metaphysics as the 'obstinate attempt to think clearly.' *It's Debatable* is metaphysical, then, but it is also deeply practical. Robert Jensen addresses the most challenging conflicts today ... [H]e distinguishes carefully and convincingly between what is real, and can therefore be considered true, and what is delusional: the result of passionately wishful or willfully ideological thinking. In a world of multiple cascading crises, *It's Debatable* thus offers a powerful case for, and demonstration of, a sane way forward. What could be more important?"
—**Patrick Curry, author of** *Ecological Ethics: An Introduction* **and editor of** *The Ecological Citizen*

"*It's Debatable* is a profound and honest dive into the challenges of our politically charged and information-saturated world ... I highly recommend this book to all. *It's Debatable* is an illuminating and captivating read, challenging us to transcend the tribalism of our times. Robert Jensen's insightful exploration of free thought, responsible speech, and authentic living is an indispensable guide for navigating today's intricate social and political terrain. This book invites us to embrace uncertainty, question our beliefs, and, above all, stay true to ourselves and our values."
—**Narissra M. Punyanunt-Carter, Department of Communication Studies, Texas Tech University, co-author of** *Interpersonal Communication: A Mindful Approach to Relationships*

IT'S DEBATABLE:

TALKING AUTHENTICALLY ABOUT TRICKY TOPICS

ROBERT JENSEN

OLIVE
BRANCH
PRESS

An imprint of Interlink Publishing Group, Inc.
Northampton, Massachusetts

First published in 2024 by

Olive Branch Press
An imprint of Interlink Publishing Group, Inc.
46 Crosby Street, Northampton, MA 01060
www.interlinkbooks.com

Library of Congress Cataloging-in-Publication data available
ISBN-13: 978-1-62371-684-4

Printed and bound in the United States of America

"However unwillingly a person who has a strong opinion may admit the possibility that his opinion may be false, he ought to be moved by the consideration that, however true it may be, if it is not fully, frequently, and fearlessly discussed, it will be held as a dead dogma, not a living truth."

—John Stuart Mill, *On Liberty*

Contents

Introduction:
Where I'm Coming From

To fulfill the obligations of democratic citizenship, we have to think freely, speak responsibly, and live authentically. Those are high standards, difficult to meet in any era. But particularly in a time marked by intense political partisanship—distorted by disembodied political engagement on social media—thinking freely, speaking responsibly, and living authentically can be a struggle.

That's partly because of our inescapable human limitations—we never know as much about the world as we would like to know, and we don't know our own motivations as well as we tend to believe we do. The world is often a mystery, and just as often we are a mystery to ourselves. We operate with incomplete information, always facing the temptation of self-serving self-delusion.

Complicating these limits is the human tendency to conform to the views of the social groups in which we anchor our sense of self. That's most obviously a problem for people in cults, although the line between a cult and what we take to be a normal social group can be hard to identify at times. (I'm kidding, sort of.) However cultish our particular groups, we all are social animals—we don't think, speak, or live alone. We don't construct the frameworks we use to navigate the world by ourselves, and we often rely on the conclusions of others who have expertise—or at least claim expertise—in areas that baffle us. Given the rapid expansion of human knowledge in the era of modern science, being routinely baffled is part of the modern condition.

Being part of groups gives us a sense of belonging and often a sense of collective power. For most of us, going along with our crowd makes us feel good, and we are reluctant to break ranks. The threat of being cast out of a group is a powerful motivator to accept beliefs, even when we have our doubts. Some people like to think they are beyond such pressures, deriding the conformists as "sheeple" who operate intellectually like domesticated animals. If we separate ourselves from crowds that we have been part of and challenge the belief systems of our peers, it's tempting to think of ourselves as operating outside the influence of a crowd. But even the crankiest contrarians are never really thinking on their own.

In my five decades of life in and around journalism, academia, and politics, I have never met anyone who thought alone. Throughout history there have been trailblazers, of course, people who have pushed beyond existing thinking to generate new ideas. But if contrarians believe they have special status—if they indulge the illusion of having risen above the collective thinking process—they are failing to practice the critical self-reflection that is supposed to be a core attribute of contrarians.

We are herd animals, and we often unthinkingly think as a herd. The fancy term for this is "identity-protective cognition," the tendency of individuals to resolve disputed facts in a manner supportive of their group identities.[1] We are motivated to adopt those beliefs to signal that we belong. Here's another fancy term: "cultural cognition of risk," our tendency to form beliefs about dangers to society that are consistent with our value judgments about what constitutes an ideal society.[2] We are motivated to assess the facts about potentially dangerous behaviors in ways that support policies we already endorse. Both of these are forms of what is often called "motivated reasoning," when our biases lead us to a particular conclusion or decision, often without any conscious awareness.

But the herd isn't always right, and we are often not very good at assessing risk. No group of people is infallible, just as no individual is infallible, and different herds can have mutually exclusive notions of how to understand a situation, which means at least one herd in such a debate is wrong, in part or totally. None of this should surprise anyone. As three scholars of language and intelligence explain, human learning is creative, which means:

[A]ny human-style explanation is not necessarily correct; we are fallible. But this is part of what it means to think: To be right, it must be possible to be wrong. Intelligence consists not only of creative conjectures but also of creative criticism. Human-style thought is based on possible explanations and error correction, a process that gradually limits what possibilities can be rationally considered.[3]

Because we are fallible, it's best that in our herds we encourage each other to stay sharp. In the smallest herds to which we belong—groups that usually are defined by shared values and tastes—we should reward people for speaking up to challenge the presumed wisdom of the herd. We should encourage lively internal debate. If we're successful at cultivating that virtue in smaller circles, we can encourage it in more diverse groups, where disagreements are likely more contentious.

I am a herd animal, no different than anyone else. Because of early experience of not fitting into "normal" social groups (that's a long story about a weird kid), I developed a contrarian streak. But I am always aware that I don't think alone. All that said, I am eager to offer the conclusions I've reached about contemporary issues with confidence, even when—perhaps especially when—members of my herd disagree.

Here's a quick summary of my evaluation of contemporary herds: I think the right-wing herd is misguided more often than it is correct, but I agree with some elements of a truly conservative worldview, especially the recognition that we humans and our systems aren't perfectible. I think the left-wing herd is correct most of the time, but my preference for leftist conclusions does not lead me to always accept the conventional wisdom of the left, which I believe is sometimes misguided.

That's enough background to make my intentions in this book clear: I will critique right-wing ideology, and I will point out what I believe to be failures of my left-leaning comrades, all the time trying to be as open as possible to critique from all sides, with the least amount of self-righteousness possible.

Like everyone, I think with others, and yet I'm responsible for defending my conclusions. Like everyone, I should work to get better at acquiring and analyzing information, as well as cultivating honest introspection. Acknowledging our intellectual interdependence in making our way through the world—even celebrating it, since I can't imagine living a truly solitary intellectual life—doesn't negate the equally obvious fact that I am an individual with a capacity to follow my own judgments in thinking, speaking, and acting.

I am not an island unto myself, and yet I recognize that there are times I may reject what others on the island believe to be true.

It makes no sense to declare myself to be the captain of my own intellectual ship and ignore the wisdom of the crew. But neither does it make sense to blow whichever way the social winds take me.

OK, enough with the mixed metaphors. Back to plain language.

Because I know that I sometimes will be wrong, I appreciate someone telling me, "Your argument is unsound and here's why." Because I know others sometimes will be wrong, I am skeptical when someone tells me, "It's wrong for you to make that argument and I won't listen." I have run into that latter response more often in the past decade of my intellectual and political life than in previous decades, which is a large part of my motivation to write this book.

AUTHENTICITY

As diligently as we may study the world and reflect on our motivations, as staunchly as we may vow not to just follow the crowd, it's not easy to think freely, speak responsibly, and live authentically.

That last term is especially hard. I mean "authenticity" not in the sense of adherence to an original, not the quest to act in accordance with a revered tradition, whether real or mythical. That kind of search for the authentic—the belief there is a "true" practice or form validated by the unquestioned superiority of tradition—is an abandonment of our responsibility to deal with a changing world. I am using "authentic" here in the sense of being true to our own professed values, that struggle to be the person we claim to be, yearn to be. That is what my late friend Abe Osheroff meant when he so often spoke of his struggle to live an authentic life, to integrate his thinking, talking, and acting.

I met Abe through our mutual involvement in the antiwar movement and progressive political organizing more generally. Already in his eighties when I met him (he died in 2008 at the age of ninety-two), Abe began his political activism during his teenage years in Brooklyn during the Great Depression. He had been a labor organizer, had traveled to Spain to fight in that country's civil war, and was involved in radical politics the rest of his life.

Abe didn't write much, and so I recorded an extended interview with him in 2005,[4] which led to a documentary film about his activism.[5] After noticing that he often invoked authenticity, I asked him what he meant by the term. Here's his answer from that interview:

> Authenticity is incredibly important. To me, authenticity comes when your thoughts, your words, and your deeds have some relation to each other. It comes when there's a real organic relationship between the way you think, the way you talk, and the way you act. You have to fight for authenticity all the time in this world, and if you don't fight for it you will get derailed. But when you have it, when you feel that surge of recognition—that I'm saying exactly what I'm thinking, and I'm ready to do something about it.
>
> Some people are afraid to think, because thinking can present problems. When you have thoughts, you have to decide what to do with them. We can save them and take them to a therapist, or we can go to a bar and drink them away, or we can talk about them. But immediately we have to deal with self-censorship. Talking honestly can have consequences. Take an easy example. If you're involved in a relationship and there's something bothering you about the relationship, and you tell the other person your thoughts, that may be the end of the relationship. You're in a funny bind because if you talk about it you may risk the relationship, but if you don't talk about it you know that down the road the same problem will be there. What do you do? Authenticity is about making that decision.
>
> Then once you've said something, the question is, "What are you going to do about it?" A lot of people don't do anything. Trying to be authentic is another way of saying you are struggling to let out the best part of who you are, the part that will act and take risks. We

all have a choice: We can choose to be made by history, or we can choose to participate in making history.

This book is my attempt to be as authentic as possible. Because it's arrogant to tell others how they should think, speak, and act, I'm offering no such advice. Rather than pretend I have it all figured out, I want to write about how I've struggled to figure it out in my own life, and why I have confidence in the things I think I have figured out.

This is not false modesty—there are some things I think I do well and some things I realize I'm not particularly good at. From an early age, growing up in North Dakota, I excelled at shoveling snow. Now in my sixties and living in northern New Mexico, I still take pride in my shoveling prowess and have expanded my skill set to include digging irrigation ditches. I also am a clear and concise writer, and I believe I became a pretty good college teacher. I have had some success in my life—I retired as a full professor from the University of Texas at Austin and have published a number of books—and I've tried to reflect honestly on the reasons for that success, beyond the obvious (that is, lots of dumb luck and being born white and male in the United States during economic boom times).

MEDIOCRITY AND STUBBORNNESS

Here's what I've concluded: The secret of my success is that I'm mediocre, and I know it.

That's what I told many of the graduate students I worked with at UT. I didn't mean that I was unqualified for my job but rather that I tried not to overestimate my abilities. In academic life, people tend to scramble around trying to prove how smart they are. Because graduate students often mimic the behavior of faculty members, I wanted them to realize that there was a path forward that didn't require them to overdrive their headlights.

I learned that lesson from a trusted friend, the late Jim Koplin,[6] who told me that one could thrive in university life without pretending to be the smartest person in the room. My intellectual deficiencies are too numerous to list in full here, but among them are a tin ear for languages (I'm monolingual), a severely limited capacity for math beyond algebra (I washed out of calculus in high school and was too lazy to try again), and an embarrassingly superficial knowledge of core sciences such as physics (please don't ask me to explain the general theory of relativity). I'll leave an evaluation of my emotional intelligence to others.

While I was working on my PhD, Jim told me, kindly but bluntly, that I lacked the background in math and science I should have; that at my age I was unlikely to make much progress in those areas; and that these weaknesses would limit the research I was competent to do. That was one of many things he was right about.

But Jim also helped me understand what I could be good at, such as distinguishing between important and trivial research in the social sciences and humanities, and then translating the best of it into plain language for students and the general public. He encouraged me to write honestly about my experience living with unearned privilege, incorporating critical self-reflection into radical analyses.

I'm mediocre. Not only do I know it, but I'm kind of proud of it, of how I have worked hard to maximize my limited abilities. Instead of always trying to puff up myself, I found ways to do what I did best within those limitations, aware that I wasn't creating new knowledge but helping others learn. Thanks to a lot of luck, I was able to build a successful professional career and also use those skills in political writing, public speaking, and community organizing.

That explains why I have the opportunity to write *a* book. Another trait of mine explains why I'm writing *this* book: I'm stubborn.

I hope my stubbornness is not the pathological kind, the annoying tendency we humans have to refuse to change our minds *even when* presented with incontrovertible evidence that we are wrong. I want to believe I am stubborn in the good sense, not abandoning a reasonable position I hold *until* someone presents such evidence. Like everyone, sometimes I have been stubborn in that embarrassing fashion. But as I have gotten older, I think I'm clearer about the difference between digging in for the sake of staying dug in, and holding one's ground because intellectual standards matter. I like to think I'm stubborn the right way.

I am mediocre and stubborn, proudly.

I realize that this may not be the smartest strategy for an introduction. So, I might as well keep digging this hole by telling a story about my own failure to live up to the standards I want to defend in this book.

In 2022, Wes Jackson and I published *An Inconvenient Apocalypse: Environmental Collapse, Climate Crisis, and the Fate of Humanity,*[7] a book about dealing with today's "multiple cascading ecological crises," a phrase I had borrowed from Jim Koplin many years before.[8] One of the "Four Hard Questions" that Wes and I take on in that book is overpopulation, asking a question that no one can answer definitively but is crucial to ask: What is the sustainable size of the human population, at what level of aggregate consumption? (If you don't want to read the book, our answer is "fewer and less," fewer people consuming a lot less, which I'll explain in Chapter 6.)

I was talking to a friend about how so many people on the left side of the political fence refuse to acknowledge that the question is relevant. Standard left dogma is that the problem is not population but capitalism—if the world's resources were distributed equitably, there would be enough for everyone. This dodge—it's economics not population—is a serious deficiency of left analysis, I told my friend, because it avoids coming to terms with the biophysical limits of the larger living world of which we are but one part.

Brief uncomfortable pause.

"When I asked you about population a long time ago," my friend said, "you told me that it wasn't important. Your answer was that the problem was capitalism. You gave me what you are now calling left dogma."

Another brief uncomfortable pause.

I had two possible responses. I could construct some tortured explanation of how my past comments were more nuanced and that what I had really meant was ...

I spared us both that torture and agreed. Yes, I said, you're absolutely right. For a long time, I repeated that dogma, even though I was never sure it made sense. I didn't challenge the claim because I hadn't read widely enough or spent enough time thinking about the question, and so I said what people of my political leanings were supposed to say. I stuck with the herd. I wanted to be seen as a good leftist, and that was lazy. Reasonable people can disagree about the issue, but accepting dogma to avoid thinking is bad intellectual practice and contributes to bad public policy. In other words, I *may* be wrong about my conclusion today, but I *definitely* was wrong simply to repeat the party line for so long.

This story demonstrates two of my deepest insights about people: We are fallible, and we don't like being fallible.

OK, those aren't deep insights. They are banal observations—banal but important reminders of why honest arguments are necessary if we are to deepen our understanding of the world. Honest arguments are most productive when we commit to thinking freely, speaking responsibly, and acting authentically; when we do our best as individuals to uphold intellectual standards; and when we recognize that upholding those standards is as much a collective as an individual effort.

We all are responsible for cultivating these intellectual, moral, and political virtues in ourselves. But we need a little help not just from our friends but also from our enemies. That can be hard these days—not just finding a way to talk to enemies but also being honest with friends.

A NOTE ON TERMINOLOGY

So far, I have invoked a right/left political framework rather than a conservative/liberal one, which I hope will minimize confusion throughout the book. But confusion is inevitable.

Take the word "liberal," which is a component of the terms "classical liberalism," "New Deal liberalism," and "neoliberalism"—three very different political formations. The term is also used as a modifier, such as a "liberal internationalist," someone committed to building a world order based on principle not power. These days, the antonym "illiberal" is used to describe authoritarian leaders who manipulate democratic systems to produce undemocratic ends. Without shared definitions, these terms can confuse more than clarify.

A leading liberal political philosopher suggests that "liberal" makes most sense as an adjective that captures a spirit best described in moral rather than political or cultural terms:

We [liberals] are, or we aspire to be, open-minded, generous, and tolerant. We are able to live with ambiguity; we are ready for arguments that we don't feel we have to win. Whatever our ideology, whatever our religion, we are not dogmatic; we are not fanatics.[9]

This book embraces those liberal values, but I am a leftist (not a liberal) who is rooted in radical (not liberal) feminism. So, what am I?

That question can be hard to answer when there are no stable, widely agreed upon definitions. A politician such as Nancy Pelosi, the former Speaker of the House of Representatives, might be described by her Democratic Party supporters as a liberal, while people further to the left might consider her to be a moderate. Meanwhile, conservative opponents routinely tagged her as far left.

For purposes of this book, I will try to stick with definitions that are most commonly used in contemporary US politics. From my perspective, the contemporary right in the United States includes openly fascistic, reactionary, and moderate versions. In the center are, well, centrists. On the left we find liberals, progressives, and leftists.

The fascistic right includes those who openly call for the United States to be a white, Christian nation and hold strong patriarchal views and a weak commitment to democracy.[10] The reactionary right includes those who believe any capitulation to democratic socialism, multiculturalism, or internationalism will destroy the country. The moderate right is the rest of the Republican Party, those who are skeptical of any restraint on the business community and are committed to US supremacy, whether it be through intervention or isolation.

Liberals offer a tempered critique of concentrated power, endorsing reforms to capitalism that include greater opportunities for women and non-white people within the existing systems. Progressives have a deeper critique of those systems but tend to be pragmatic and avoid calls for radical change. Leftists argue that we must abandon those systems and find new ways of organizing the economy and international order, typically around socialist principles.

Who does that leave in the center? People who are uncomfortable with too much change too quickly, those willing to accept most any policy proposal that promises stability and protects the status quo.

In this summary, I have not included positions on the ecological crises, which don't always map easily onto left/right frameworks, though in general the left side of the fence takes those crises more seriously than the right. But as I'll argue in Chapter 6, the differences in right and left on these matters may not be as important as their unacknowledged points of agreement.

At times I'll talk about right and left in general ways, recognizing that there are important distinctions within those groupings but that for certain purposes the binary is adequate. When the distinctions are more central to any analysis, I'll mark them.

Chapter 1:
Stepping Up: Contemporary Controversies

The past three decades in the United States have been a time of increasing political polarization, particularly since the 2016 presidential election. In addition to the tensions across political parties and ideologies, sharp internal conflicts have emerged in recent years. Traditional conservatives have struggled with more extremist formations on the right that promote baseless conspiracy theories and reject the most basic democratic principle: a commitment to accept the results of elections. Meanwhile, liberal/progressive/left people have struggled with how to deal with disagreements within their movements, particularly on issues involving race and the sex/gender system.

Is this a unique time in US history? That's hard to argue in a country that experienced decades of intense political conflict over slavery that often turned violent, culminating in a bloody civil war in which more than six hundred thousand people died. Then there were the two major Red Scares in the twentieth century, labor actions that were met with violence from employers and governments, an intensifying civil rights movement starting in the 1950s, the anti-Vietnam War movement of the 1960s, and the feminist movement emerging in the same period. These were all times when some people wanted revolutionary change while others were willing to do most anything to prevent it, and society was fractured along lines of age, race, sex, economics, and ideology.

But that shouldn't make us feel upbeat. Just because there were troubled periods in the past doesn't make today's polarization trivial, especially because it is happening at a unique time, in ecological terms. Remember those "multiple cascading crises"? Rapid climate destabilization[11] is the most recent of those crises, and perhaps the most devastating, but we also have to deal with soil erosion and degradation,[12] chemical contamination of ecosystems and our bodies,[13] and species extinction and loss of biodiversity as the result of human expansion.[14]

Crises are not new, of course. Over the past few thousand years, we have faced regional ecological catastrophes, the fall of empires, and world wars. But never before have we faced global ecological collapse. And at this moment when we need an all-hands-on-deck united effort, we are dealing with a breakdown of the economic (capitalism) and political (liberal democracy) systems that many assumed were stable. "The end of history," a post-Cold War term to describe the presumed victory of liberal capitalist democracy over other ideologies, has given way to increasing fear of the literal end of human history.

Facing such dire circumstances, it's tempting to argue that we should forgo ideological debate in favor of practical solutions, focusing on whatever works. Every few years, political centrists float the idea of a party[15] for those who are committed to solving problems without getting bogged down in ideological clashes, as if different proposed solutions don't come from ideological positions and don't favor some people's priorities and ignore others. Arguing that we should put aside ideology is, in the end, a parlor trick to get others to accept your ideology.

I am strongly in favor of continuing to talk, not just to rehash ideological disagreements—which do need constant rehashing—but also to examine how different ideological perspectives affect our perceptions of reality. The goal is not intellectual one-upmanship but helping one another see how our various perspectives both illuminate and limit, so that we get better at solving disagreements by using evidence and logic. If such talking never led to action, we would have a problem. But if action goes forward without such talking, we have a different kind of problem. Actions that are rooted in a misunderstanding of the nature of crises are unlikely to lead to productive policies.

Take the current conversation about the ecological crises as an example. Many environmentalists are focused on climate change, which is easy to understand as Earth warms and the catastrophic consequences become undeniable. One proposed solution is to decarbonize the economy by replacing fossil fuels with renewable energy sources and capturing carbon emissions for storage. Other environmentalists argue that climate change is a derivative of the more fundamental problem of overshoot—too many people, consuming too much in the aggregate, exhausting the regenerative capacity of the ecosphere. Which framework is the most accurate account of reality? That's not an abstract question for a debating society. How we resolve the questions will influence what kind of policies we enact and how effective those policies are likely to be.

Action is impossible without thinking and talking. Everything we do is based on some idea of how the world works, ideas that we almost always have discussed with others. And the thinking and talking continue after we have decided what to do in that moment; the decision to take an action doesn't end the process of understanding the world. (More on all this in chapters 2 and 3.)

Discussions about a complex world are bound to be contentious, inevitably leading to conflict. In a healthy society, people (especially journalists, writers, teachers, and researchers who are paid to do intellectual work) would not only accept the inevitability of debate but encourage it.[16] In a healthy society, institutions (especially mass media, think tanks, schools, and universities) would provide spaces and resources for managing the conflict to make it as productive as possible.

I'm not sure I have ever lived in a healthy society.

POLITICAL CORRECTNESS AND CULTURE WARS

When I started my career as a professor in 1992, the buzzwords that captured intellectual and political tensions were "political correctness"[17] and "culture wars."[18] The right decried the political correctness of the left. The left condemned the right for fomenting culture wars. Both phrases generated more heat than light, more political bluster than insight. Both terms can be defined in a positive or negative fashion. Both types of definitions are accurate in certain ways.

What is political correctness, and is it a good thing? If the term means, for example, that most mainstream institutions in the United States—a society that has long been dominated by white-supremacist ideology—have decreed that racist slurs are unacceptable, then political correctness is a good thing. While white-supremacist attitudes haven't disappeared, an agreement to reject such slurs in conversation is a sign of progress. But it's also true that the overly harsh policing of speech can undermine the robust discussion essential to intellectual engagement and democratic politics. Rushing to judgment about the motives of others, which inevitably happens in such an atmosphere, quickly can lead to anger and recrimination rather than open up potential for collaboration. In those situations, political correctness is counterproductive.

What are culture wars, and are they destructive? If the term describes the deep divides in US society about such things as the role of religious faith in public life, then it's simply a description of one aspect of political life. Maybe the "war" metaphor is hyperbolic (although wars have been fought over religion throughout history), but some policy conflicts are unavoidable. Should a city allow space in a public park to be used for sectarian religious displays? That's a real public-policy question on which reasonable people can disagree. On the other hand, if there is a trend among businesses that serve customers of diverse faiths to welcome them in December with "Happy Holidays" instead of "Merry Christmas," is that really a threat to Christianity? Whipping up hysteria about a "war on Christmas" is unproductive culture warfare, designed not to resolve a conflict but to fuel a sense of victimhood.

These kinds of issues in the 1990s produced lots of conflict, some inevitable in a multicultural democracy and some created for partisan political advantage. Again, perspective is necessary—political and social conflicts of varying intensity run all through US history. The social ferment that peaked in the 1960s generated a lot of conflict that was inevitable given conflicting values and goals. We need not pretend that our public discourse is at an unprecedented low point to recognize the need to raise intellectual standards in the service of more productive political conversation.

And what of our experience in the twenty-first century? Have things gotten better or worse?

WOKENESS AND CANCEL CULTURE

Today, "political correctness" and the "culture wars" are still in circulation, but two new terms dominate the conversation about controversial topics: "wokeness" and "cancel culture." In general, people on the right use the terms to describe what they believe to be liberal/progressive/left overreach, arguing that wokeness and cancel culture are destructive forces undermining bedrock American values and freedoms. In general, people on the left argue that those terms are rhetorical weapons that reactionary movements use to distract the public from understanding how systems of power and contemporary institutions undermine human dignity.

I don't pretend to be neutral in these matters. I come from the left with a longstanding focus on white supremacy (more on that in Chapter 4), anchored in radical feminism (not liberal or postmodern feminism, a distinction that will be central in Chapter 5), with an ecological worldview (not an industrial worldview, a distinction I'll take up in Chapter 6). My assessment is that right-wing politicians and political strategists are irresponsible in their use of these terms, in most cases to attract and motivate supporters. The right is weaponizing these terms more than the left, most notably in right-wing hysteria about the teaching of critical race theory. But the left often goes off the rails as well, sometimes abandoning commitments to intellectual standards and political principles, such as in the debate over transgender ideology.

To be crystal clear: I am *not* saying I believe that right and left are equally destructive. I am not engaging in false equivalency in the hope of appearing measured and moderate. I have spent more than three decades developing a critical politics rooted in left analyses of systems and structures of power, and I am not backpedaling from those positions.

If anything, the older I get the more radical I get. My critique of the right is motivated by a fear of unsound arguments, ugly emotions, and destructive politics. My critique of the left is motivated by a desire to advance the radical analyses I believe are crucial to human thriving, analyses that can be undermined by overly zealous activists.

Said differently, I critique right-wing ideology because it is at odds with my values, and I believe it to be harmful. I critique left-wing ideology in an attempt to strengthen left analyses, which I believe to be essential. No matter what my motivations, both activities have landed me in trouble. When I have written about racism and white supremacy, I have been accused by the right of being woke. As a result of my writing about sex/gender and patriarchy, I have been canceled by the left.

Being denounced by a variety of political actors doesn't prove that one is insightful. "The right hates me and the left hates me, and so I must be onto something" is a shabby defense. I don't expect people to pay attention to my work because I've been attacked. All I ask is that people evaluate my arguments on intellectual grounds—that is, assessing the evidence and logic used to reach conclusions—rather than simply denouncing the ideas without serious examination and rebuttal.

I try not to take either the accusations of wokeness or the canceling personally. My primary concern is about the way intellectual inquiry and political debate can be constrained and degraded in this atmosphere.

Let's start with definitions. I like to start with definitions, mostly because I see too many debates going forward with little clarity on how terms are used. Perhaps it's impossible to create much order in a chaotic world, but I see no alternative to doing our best to define terms in the hope of imposing some order on unruly debaters.

STAYING WOKE

Does "woke" mean staying aware of social injustices such as racism, remaining vigilant and attentive to the need for constant struggle? Huddie William Ledbetter, the folk/blues performer better known as Lead Belly, thought so. Discussing his song "Scottsboro Boys,"[19] he advised black people to "stay woke" to the violent realities of white supremacy, especially in places such as Alabama, where those nine boys and young men accused of rape in 1931 escaped a lynching but found themselves railroaded by a racist court system. "I advise everybody to be a little careful when they go down through there," Lead Belly said of Alabama. "Just stay woke. Keep your eyes open."[20] That's widely considered to be the origin of the term, long before it was bandied about in the dominant culture.

Or, does "woke" describe the attempt by people on the left to impose their ideology on everyone else, either through public policy or pressure on private institutions and businesses? That's how conservatives have redefined the term, usually with some contempt and derision[21] toward those they accuse of "virtue signaling,"[22] publicly displaying their wokeness to demonstrate their presumed moral superiority.

Both definitions can be accurate, depending on the situation.

We can understand wokeness in a positive sense, following Lead Belly. Should people who are on the bottom of various social hierarchies stay woke? That certainly seems sensible, given the way people in power so often work to maintain those hierarchies, sometimes while at the same time pledging to pursue the goal of equity. Should a black driver who gets stopped by a police officer be awake to patterns of the disproportionate use of force against African Americans? That seems like good advice, not because all cops are abusive in every encounter but because some people are at greater risk. And if vulnerable people should stay woke out of self-interest, it would be appropriate for people in dominant positions in the hierarchies to strive to be woke out of solidarity.

What about wokeness in a negative sense? Do people who consider themselves to be woke ever behave in overly zealous ways when they apply their analysis of hierarchy and oppression to situations in their lives? Almost everyone, especially those of us who have spent time on college campuses over the past decade, can tell a story about such zealousness undermining productive conversations. For example, I've heard the phrase "check your privilege"—intended as a reminder to people with unearned advantages to be self-reflective—used in ways that shut down engagement rather than open up an exchange. In practice, "check your privilege" can be wielded as a synonym for "shut up."

Here's an example of the complexity that will be familiar to many readers. During a meeting, some participants will preface a statement with phrases such as "As an indigenous man," or "As a black woman." Sometimes those details help others understand their comment, but some speakers use their identity to suggest that critique from white people or men, or both, is out of bounds and that their analysis is beyond challenge. Experience matters in how we understand the world, but it doesn't guarantee one has the best argument. As I repeatedly told students, their experience may be the starting point for an analysis, but simply recounting their experience isn't an analysis. If those kind of identity invocations shut down a conversation, everyone loses. That doesn't mean that hierarchies don't exist or that oppression is acceptable. It simply recognizes that some people can derail important conversations by implicitly claiming that some other people cannot challenge their statements.

If this critique seems suspect coming from a white man, consider the analysis of Maurice Mitchell, national director of the Working Families Party, which describes him as "a nationally recognized social movement strategist, a visionary leader in the Movement for Black Lives, and a community organizer for racial, social, and economic justice." In an essay widely circulated on the left, Mitchell was blunt: "Identity and position are misused to create a doom loop that can lead to unnecessary ruptures of our political vehicles and the shuttering of vital movement spaces."[23] On a podcast after the essay was published, he said he has seen identity "being weaponized in ways that were not useful for the work." He elaborated:

> As a black person, it does no favors to me for me to say, "As a black son of immigrants," and then for white people to sit on their hands and shut up. I need to be sharpened by debate. I might, at the end of the day, think you're wrong. But I need the back and forth in order to sharpen my position or change my mind.[24]

Where does this leave us? Let's take the case of race. Some on the right say that racism is no longer a powerful force shaping people's options.

Most on the left argue that racist practices continue, albeit in different forms than in previous eras, and must be addressed in public policy. (I say "most," because some leftists argue that class divisions in capitalism are primary, both in terms of analysis and action.)

Let's start with potential points of agreement. Everyone should be able to agree that the United States, both in legal and informal ways, has made progress in confronting white supremacy and changing racist practices. Would anyone argue that the United States in 2024 is no different than it was in the pre-civil rights twentieth century? I think of this in concrete terms, about the year I was born. Does anyone—anyone who isn't an overt racist, that is—want to return to the racial dynamics of 1958?

Yet it's also true that racialized disparities in measures of wealth and well-being—the statistics that tell us roughly how well people are doing—continue even after changes in law and policy.[25] Given the racist history of the United States and the recent resurgence of open white-supremacist rhetoric, would anyone argue that we have transcended white supremacy in the few decades since the end of legal apartheid? Does anyone want to freeze racial dynamics at this moment in history because it can't get any better than this?

How do we sort this out? Too often, too many white people want to deny the lingering racist patterns in virtually every aspect of American life. When those white people are quick to label antiracist activists as overly zealous, that might be part of a denial strategy. It's fair to ask whether critiques of wokeness might sometimes be a way to divert attention from the enduring nature of white supremacy.

Yet it's also reasonable to worry that such zealousness sometimes undermines the difficult work of building coalitions that can advance an antiracist agenda. People with a perceptive critique of white supremacy are people, and people can be arrogant in all sorts of ways. For example, the line between holding someone accountable for a racist comment and berating a well-intentioned person who may not be up-to-date on the latest trends in progressive terminology can be pretty thin. Even the director of a university's Africana studies program can find himself undermined by a self-righteous student who feels the professor isn't taking the correct position.[26] If all these points are reasonable, then the only way forward is to acknowledge these complex social realities and step back from the polarizing platitudes. Reasonable people on the right should be able to acknowledge that white supremacy is a dangerous part of conservative political formations today. Reasonable people on the left should be able to acknowledge that it is better to present arguments based on evidence and logic rather than merely to denounce political opponents who don't share their views on race.

Vincent Lloyd, the Africana studies professor who saw that seminar he was teaching undermined, offers a perceptive analysis of the situation:

> I worry that left political discourse today takes social movements, or even just an individual who has suffered, as conversation stoppers rather than conversation starters. That frustrates me because I firmly believe these movements are the key to our collective liberation. Justice struggles always involve a back-and-forth between movement participants making demands for radical transformation and those in power trying to manage those demands so that they can keep their grip on power. ... Those of us who care about justice have to be willing to ask critical questions about these dynamics rather than blindly deferring to the activist language.[27]

CANCEL CULTURE

A variety of terms exist to describe the process of disciplining someone for a perceived political or moral offense: shunning (refusing to associate with someone and encouraging others to do the same), canceling (removing someone from a position), or de-platforming (curtailing someone's ability to speak in some public setting). Who gets canceled and how it plays out will depend on the public visibility of the person, the issue in question, and the power of the people doing the disciplining.

Context is crucial. Sometimes people who complain that they have been canceled have simply been critiqued in perfectly appropriate ways by people with whom they disagree. But sometimes people who say they have been canceled have been treated unfairly simply for holding a political position not favored in a group. Again, some definitional clarity is in order.

Within a political or social group with a mission and shared values, no one doubts that the group should enforce certain ideological baselines. Let's start with a playful example. Several friends establish a chess club. A person who hates chess (perhaps a fanatical parent harangued this poor child to play constantly, resulting in a pathological anti-chess attitude) joins the club to disrupt others' enjoyment of the game. No one would say that expelling the chess-hater from the club would be an inappropriate act of canceling, even if the person were an exceptional chess player. The group exists for a specific reason, which poses no threat to anyone outside the group, and disrupting the group serves no positive purpose.

Let's move to a more realistic example. Imagine a community group is engaged in progressive political organizing on an issue such as militarism, economic justice, or environmental protection. If a member of the group consistently makes racist or sexist comments, should the group discipline or expel the offender? The first step might be to confront the person in a way that seeks resolution—"calling in" (reaching out to the person who has engaged in inappropriate behavior for dialogue) rather than "calling out" (publicly challenging or shaming them).[28] But if the offender refuses to reconsider and argues that views on race and sex/gender are irrelevant to the group's focus, must the group accept that individual?

It's difficult to argue for inclusion, on at least two grounds. First, such comments can create a hostile environment that makes it difficult for others to participate. Second, even if the group includes only white men, a racist or sexist politics that accepts hierarchy on those fronts can't be squared with a progressive challenge to hierarchy and abuse on other fronts. On the left side of the fence, no one tries to offer an intellectual defense of racism or sexism.

Things get trickier in more public realms, especially when the power of governments is in play. In US law, the dominant interpretation of the First Amendment's protection of free speech and press provides wide latitude for citizens. But when an individual is acting on behalf of a public institution, where duties are as important as rights, things get murkier. Should a professor at a public university be disciplined for making openly racist comments in class? Context is relevant, but if such comments create a hostile environment that deprives some students of the education they are there to get, discipline would be appropriate.[29] What about a professor who pursues research on intelligence that some people believe to be either overtly racist or motivated by unconscious racism? Again, context matters, but that professor can claim academic freedom.

And then there are the cases from mass media and pop culture. What price should individuals in the public eye pay for actions that are deemed inappropriate in some way? First, we have to distinguish between inappropriateness and illegal behavior. Hollywood producer Harvey Weinstein was not canceled for being inappropriate. He was a serial sexual predator who was eventually convicted of rape. Fox News commentator Bill O'Reilly was dropped by the network after news leaked that he had settled five lawsuits filed by women accusing him of sexual harassment and misconduct. Prosecutors go after criminals. Corporations fire employees who violate work rules or expose the firm to damages for abusive behavior. Behavior that is illegal or creates serious legal liability is well outside discussions of cancel culture.

But other cases are more vexing, sometimes involving actions decades before, sometimes involving jokes that were acceptable in the dominant culture at the time, or actions that the perpetrator has admitted to and apologized for. Consider these cases: A white politician who appeared in blackface while in medical school, and a male politician accused of making sexist jokes and inappropriate touching while hugging supporters. Neither was accused of holding racist or sexist views in the present or pursuing racist or sexist political agendas. The former (Ralph Northam, the governor of Virginia) stayed in office and served out his term without incident. The latter (Al Franken, the US senator from Minnesota) resigned under pressure, a decision that he, along with some who had demanded his resignation, later regretted. Like-minded people can, and in these cases did, disagree.

To repeat, context is everything. When an apology for racist or sexist comments seems sincere, should offenders be treated differently than those who won't acknowledge wrongdoing? In cases where evidence is not conclusive, how do we balance a desire to protect people from abuse with the need for fairness in fact-finding and deliberation? Given how different people can perceive the same event in very different ways, how do we resolve such disagreements when there is no evidence beyond self-reports? Even when it is widely agreed that the alleged speech or actions are inappropriate, these factors complicate our decision-making processes.

WOKE AND CANCELED

Political outcomes aren't always determined by who has the best argument, of course. But in all aspects of our lives, including politics, we should try to maintain the best intellectual practices we can. I don't mean "intellectual" in an elitist sense that suggests those with the most advanced degrees always know best. Here, intellectual simply means the quest to understand how the world really works. Whatever we do for a living, we all engage in intellectual activity. I spent my adult life working as a journalist and a professor, two occupations in which I was paid to do intellectual work. But I also have been involved in a variety of political and community organizing efforts, in which I developed my intellectual life in association with comrades.

Some of those efforts involved a left critique of economic injustice in capitalism and opposition to US imperialism, whether through military actions or global economic dominance. On those issues, there was often disagreement about strategy and tactics in groups but broad agreement about the illegitimate nature of the economic and political systems we opposed.

There is more disagreement on the left about how to understand race and racism—often because of disagreements about the role of class and capitalism—but those disagreements tend to be civil and aim to deepen understanding. My first article about racism, explaining the concept of white privilege,[30] was published in 1998 and widely shared online. In 2005,

I published a book expanding on those ideas.[31] None of my left colleagues ever suggested that my analysis of race was out of bounds; there's a sense of shared opposition to a conservative politics that downplays the role of white supremacy in US history and contemporary policy.

But because I also am rooted in a radical feminist critique of patriarchy,[32] I am routinely at odds with left allies, especially on questions concerning the sexual-exploitation industries (pornography, prostitution, stripping, massage parlors) and transgender ideology (what is often called gender-identity theory). People on the left routinely embrace a liberal position on these issues, accepting a liberal definition of liberation as personal choice rather than a left definition of liberation as a change in an oppressive system and its institutions.

I'll say more about all this in chapters that follow. But to summarize my goal: I hope that I can present a respectful and rational approach to these questions. I will challenge both the reactionary politics of today's right-wing groups and the intellectual inconsistencies of the left.

Readers trying to fit me into conventional categories may be perplexed.

Am I woke? I have been described as part of the woke mob on racial justice, one of those people who allegedly is ashamed to be white.

I've been canceled in left spaces for my writing on patriarchy, especially my challenges to transgender ideology.

To repeat: being disliked by people on both sides of a debate isn't a guarantee that one is correct. But those experiences have prompted me to reflect on contemporary intellectual life—how we think and what the rules for speaking should be.

Chapter 2:
Stepping Back: Thinking

I make no claim to mastery of the vast philosophical literature on epistemology, the branch of philosophy that generates theories of knowledge, the inquiry into how we claim to know what we think we know. I have spent considerable time over the years teaching the philosophy of freedom of expression and First Amendment law, but even there I am hesitant to claim expert status.

Instead of pretending to have new insights about these subjects, I want to present ideas and advice about thinking and speaking that draw on my teaching and activist experiences. I taught university classes for twenty-nine years, and I have been writing and speaking in public for almost as long. The longer I engaged in those activities, the more I came to appreciate the complexity of the world, and the more focused I became on finding straightforward, jargon-free ways to capture what I have learned about all that complexity. My goal is simplicity in presentation without falling into simplistic thinking.

In scholarly research, people often move from general questions to increasingly specific inquiries. In the pursuit of big theories, scientists bear down on small parts of the puzzle, and then try to connect the dots. From there, others can connect the connected dots for a wider audience, trying to pull together the key insights of specialists. That's been my goal in the classroom and in public. I want to be a "synthesist," defined by a sociologist in the form of a help-wanted ad:

WANTED: SYNTHESIST
Qualified candidates should be adept at: recognizing complementary information and knowledge from diverse disciplines, integrating it into a unified framework, and using it to guide inquiry, facilitate communication and collaboration, and inform action on real problems. Requirements: long-term systems thinking, willingness to flout disciplinary conventions, ability to work well with others. Comes with exceptional benefits![33]

I'm not sure I am adept enough at all those things to get the job, but I am aware of one exceptional benefit that comes with the work: fun. When I was in graduate school, I met Jim Koplin, a psychology professor who had retired early to pursue full-time community service. He helped me understand that reading widely, thinking critically, and tackling difficult subjects was one of the great joys in life. For Jim, one of the most important roles for a teacher was speaking about that joy, which he believed everyone was capable of experiencing. "Open-ended, disciplined inquiry," he once wrote me, "is a lot more fun than gambling at the casino, or sitting with the Game Boy in your lap."[34] (The video game console reference dates the correspondence; he wrote that letter on March 30, 1997.)

Jim was one of the most relentlessly curious people I have ever known. Everyone who visited his house quizzed him about his current interests, reflected in the wide-ranging stack of library books on his table, from literature to the latest science. He was a great example of how a deep curiosity about science, broadly defined, can be a counterweight to our tendency to process information in ways that simply validate our existing beliefs.[35]

Jim also was willing to tackle controversial questions that might lead to disagreements with friends, and he poked at weaknesses in arguments wherever he found them. Following the terms used by the host of the Rationally Speaking podcast, Jim acted more like a scout than a soldier on the intellectual battlefield. A soldier-thinker uses information as ammunition against an enemy, while a scout-thinker surveys the landscape to create the most accurate picture possible.[36] Tune into today's political debates, and there seem to be a lot of soldiers and not nearly enough scouts.

I will try to follow Jim's example in this book. While I'm not trying to appear neutral by focusing on what I believe to be errors in arguments on all sides, readers on both the left and the right likely have already found things to dispute, and I will continue that approach in this chapter. Being self-critical, individually and collectively, is as important as critiquing opposing points of view.

KNOWLEDGE, TRUTH, NARRATIVE

I want to start our "open-ended, disciplined inquiry" by thinking about the nature of knowledge claims. Given the pressing social and ecological problems that we face today, it may seem a bit indulgent to spend much time thinking about how we claim to know. But how we understand the world certainly affects how we understand our options for acting in the world. Lazy thinking is likely to produce a distorted evaluation of options. So, I want to start by reflecting on our knowledge claims, which requires some definitions.

The traditional definition of knowledge is "justified true belief," what philosophers call the JTB account of knowledge. People can have all sorts of beliefs, many of them firmly held, that are at odds with the available evidence—simply believing something doesn't make it true. And we might hold a true belief that we stumbled onto without being able to provide a justification for it. Knowledge comes when what we believe is true and we can provide adequate reasons for holding the belief.

Again, I am not an expert and am not pretending to delve deeply into the subject. The minute that traditional definition is offered, philosophers will line up to explain why it's inadequate.[37] Got it. But justified true belief seems an adequate enough definition to move forward, to allow us to explore the important questions about how we understand the world.

We should care about setting standards for knowledge, especially in a period marked by "epistemic pluralism." We live in a society in which there is entrenched disagreement not only about values but about matters of empirical fact.[38] Hashing out our knowledge claims is hard, maybe at times impossible, but it's always necessary. Toward that end, I often quote one of my favorite radicals, the late writer/activist Scott Nearing, who set for himself this goal: "to learn the truth, to teach the truth, and to help build the truth into the life of the community."[39] In addition to the high standard Nearing set, which echoes Abe Osheroff's reflections on authenticity from the Introduction, I like his straightforward use of *the* truth. Yes, too many people too often claim to know *the* truth without justification, and there are many questions that we will never answer with *the* definitive truth. But seeking *the* truth is important in a culture in which people are encouraged to "speak *your* truth." I don't want to be cranky and get bogged down in *the*-versus-*your* truths, but it is worth a moment of our time. (Yes, this is a pet peeve of mine.)

I believe that everyone should speak about their experience and beliefs. Everyone should speak about their aspirations, their convictions, their reactions to the world. When people are angry about being mistreated, they should express their anger. We should strive for communities in which people are not afraid to speak about their lives, as honestly and bluntly as needed. If that's the intention behind "speak your truth," well, OK, but that might be better phrased as "speak honestly about your experience, emotions, and ideas."

I want to reserve the term "truth" for something more, for the product of our collective investigation into how the world works, pursued with as much rigor as possible. In graduate school in the late 1980s, I was warned by various critics of Western philosophy that speaking of "big-T truth" was arrogant, that such claims were too often a form of domination. Disparities in power certainly can skew the truth-seeking process, and people with power sometimes do impose self-serving truth claims on people without power. We should be on the lookout for such distortions, but truth is not an individual thing. We should make truth claims with input from others, with awareness of any individual's limited perspective.

So, let's stop encouraging people to "speak your truth" and instead encourage everyone to join a conversation and contribute to the best account of the truth we can manage together, knowing that account will always be open to challenge.

As long as I'm being cranky, here's one more contemporary phrase I would like to banish: "That's your narrative." The first time I heard this came when I had a dispute with a comrade in a community-organizing project. I laid out my assessment of the conflicts between our two groups, and her response was, "Well, that's your narrative." Her narrative, obviously, was different.

I know that any report of facts is assembled with a perspective, that we are all prone to a self-serving assemblage, that we have to listen to how others interpret the same experiences. But in that case, "That's your narrative" wasn't an invitation to engagement but a marker of the end of a conversation, a way of saying, "You see it your way, I see it mine, and I'm not interested in talking about it." She made it clear that she had no interest in reconciling our perspectives. Not surprisingly, the relationship between her organization and mine didn't last much longer.

Again, to be clear: It is naive to ignore the ways power and status can distort the process of collectively determining the truth and constructing a coherent narrative about the world. In that case, I was an older guy with a sort-of prestigious job, and she was a younger woman establishing a career. She might not have trusted me enough to defend her truth and her narrative to me, though based on previous interaction I don't think that was her concern—she was one of the most strong-willed people I have known and had never hesitated to be blunt with me before that. Whatever the dynamics of that particular situation, people with power can unfairly control the process of truth-determination and narrative-construction, leading to inaccurate accounts. But in addition to the distorting effects of raw power, individual self-interest and political dogma can distort a person's capacity to see the world as clearly as possible. There are both blunt and subtle ways to undermine good intellectual practice, and we all have to be on guard.

Self-indulgent talk of individuals' separate truths is a dead end, but so is capitulating to an authority's attempts to impose its truth. Both statements are relevant to fostering good intellectual practice. Perspectives shape narratives, but reconciling conflicting narratives is important. Both of those statements are relevant, too.

OBJECTIVE, SUBJECTIVE, AND INTERSUBJECTIVE

When conflicts about observations and interpretations arise, it's tempting to want to transcend the subjective and search for some source of objective knowledge that can be trusted without question. Some sources of knowledge are more trustworthy than others, of course. But human inquiry into the world is not best understood as the clash between *objective* and *subjective*, between inquiry validated from an external perspective that is unquestionably trustworthy versus that which is purely internal, personal, and potentially distorted. All knowledge construction and truth seeking is *intersubjective*,[40] which means it is always potentially messy.

Even a simple laboratory experiment requires judgments, however limited, by the experimenter. The more complex the phenomena being investigated, the more we have to talk through the various judgments we make in our inquiries. A sociologist who studies the practice of science describes it this way, and her observations also apply to our everyday lives:

> When scientific, knowledge-creating labor is divided among the members of a research group, these members come to depend upon one another. Evidence has to be gathered, arguments have to be formulated and collaborating scientists have to rely on one another for the bits and pieces of experimental evidence, interpretation and argument that are eventually to be integrated into a well-corroborated, publishable, scientific knowledge claim. As scientists form beliefs about the quality of the evidence and arguments, they crucially depend on the beliefs of their collaborators who have carried out experiments and gathered experimental data or who possess, for example, the necessary expertise to interpret the data and formulate an argument.[41]

When studying people and societies, the complexity increases. A good example of the messiness is the concept of date rape. Prior to the 1980s, there was no such thing as date rape—not because men never sexually assaulted women on dates, but because the culture had no term for it. As many women have testified, up until then "date rape" was typically understood as a "bad date," with little or no recourse available to women. How did that change? Using personal testimony (what is often considered to be subjective) and a growing body of formal research (what is often considered to be objective), a feminist movement demonstrated how common men's sexual violence against women is and how it is committed not only by strangers but more often by men whom women know, including in dating relationships. This intersubjective process—individual stories informing social science research and vice versa—provided evidence for feminist challenges to patriarchy that forced the culture to acknowledge this pattern.

This also is an example of how "your truth" and "your narrative" are inadequate. If we simply took differing male and female accounts of this sexual violence as individuals' truth and narrative, what resolution would be possible? A man might say, "We went on a date and you clearly wanted sex." A woman might say, "I made it clear I did not want sex but eventually gave in out of fear." Are they simply competing truths, alternative narratives? Not if we look at the pattern of male sexual violence in patriarchy, where we see that men consistently construct self-serving narratives designed to evade accountability.

That doesn't mean in every case we know with certainty that a woman's account is accurate and a man's account is not. The phrase "Believe women" that came out of the #MeToo movement can't mean "Believe all women all the time no matter what the situation." Instead, it can mean something like, "Women are routinely ignored or denigrated when they report sexual assault and harassment, because in patriarchy it is possible that men's claim of a right of sexual access to women can override women's accounts of abuse. Women can, and sometimes do, make false reports, but those cases are rare, and so in the absence of a compelling reason to disbelieve women, we should believe women." That's not much of a slogan, but it keeps us focused on the pattern of men's sexual exploitation of, and violence against, women when we have to evaluate conflicting accounts.

But there's another level of complexity to the story, about the problem of trusting men's and women's self-reports. In the late 1980s, at the beginning of my inquiry into these issues, I read a research report in which more than half of college women interviewed had reported being victims of some level of sexual aggression. That surprised me at the time. But more disturbing was that only 27 percent of women whose experience met the legal definition of rape labeled themselves as rape victims. Meanwhile, 88 percent of men who reported an assault that met the legal definition of rape were adamant that they had not raped, and 47 percent of the men who had raped said they expected to engage in a similar assault in the future.[42] How can we accurately estimate the prevalence and incidence of sexual violence when the self-reports of both victims and perpetrators are routinely inaccurate?

I want to believe that a similar study done today, after decades of greater awareness of men's sexual aggression, would generate patterns less chilling. But a 2017 study of male students at a large university found that 54.3 percent of athletes and 37.9 percent of non-athletes self-reported perpetrating some form of sexual coercion.[43] A 2022 study found that the problem in sexual coercion typically is not "miscommunication"—men understand women's refusals but use feigned naivete to justify and minimize the effects of their use of coercion.[44]

And women continue to report that they don't always understand an assault as being an assault. As one woman put it in a recent essay:

> It took me 12 years to realize it was rape. For more than a decade, the trauma I experienced the summer after high school stayed filed away in my brain as something to be ashamed of, something to keep secret.[45]

Also, men who are sexually violent today are more likely than in the past to offer a "rough sex" defense—the idea that women enjoy being slapped or strangled during sex, which plays into longstanding rape myths that "situate sexual violence as exceptional, frequently question women's truthfulness and suggest that claims of sexual violence are at best exaggerated and, at worst, false."[46]

From this we *should not* conclude that it's impossible to know anything about sexual assault, and we *should not* assume that all truths and narratives are equally reliable or unreliable. We *should* recognize that

42

for millennia, patriarchal ideology—the assertion that male dominance and female subordination are natural and inevitable—has normalized men's violence and sexual exploitation to such a degree that in some situations this sexual abuse can be invisible both to perpetrator and victim. This realization should spur us to create more opportunities for women to speak up, more research to understand the patterns and the ideology. We should care enough to expend the resources necessary to find out.

BACK TO TRUTH

If we invest the appropriate time and energy to understand a complex question, we still will struggle to come to our best account of the truth. Since history is littered with discarded beliefs that were once thought to be true beyond question (remember the Earth-centered solar system?), considerable humility is necessary. But we want to move toward the truth, as best we can determine it.

More definitional work is needed. What do we mean when we say we believe something to be true? There are only three possible answers.

OK, that was kind of a joke. Suggesting that any complex question in human affairs can be reduced to three choices is evidence of a lack of humility. That said, there are three main approaches to truth in Western philosophy, which cover a lot of ground: correspondence, coherence, and consensus. (To be more precise, what I'm calling a consensus theory of truth is usually called the pragmatic theory. But I like alliterative lists of three items.)

Let me repeat my standard warning: I am simplifying a complex philosophical literature in a way that non-philosophers (like me) can understand. This is not meant to exhaust the subject but to construct a sensible scaffolding on which we can operate.

- Correspondence: The truth or falsity of a statement is determined by how it relates to the world, whether it accurately describes, or corresponds to that world. A correspondence theory states that the truth claim of a proposition is determined by objective features of the world that are independent of human perception.[47]

43

- Coherence: The truth or falsity of a statement is determined by its relation to other statements rather than its relation to the world, by its coherence with a set of propositions about how the world works. A coherence theory states that the truth of a proposition comes from its connection to other propositions believed to be true.[48]
- Consensus/pragmatic: Truth is what those in a community agree is true, which is generally what works for people, what helps them solve problems and resolve disputes about how the world works.[49]

From there, another question is crucial: What do we want to know the truth about? What kinds of questions are we trying to answer? What do we need to understand, to the best of our ability, about how the world works, so that we can make the best choices possible? Once again, I'll offer a list of three (no alliteration this time).

- Empirical: We try to determine facts about the world, collecting data and describing what happens around us.
- Analytical: We examine the empirical evidence to build theories and models about how the world works.
- Normative: We want to come to judgment about how societies, governments, and economies should work, asserting norms for human behavior.[50]

Those three ideas about truth map roughly onto the three types of truth claims. When charting the empirical, we are especially interested in achieving the closest possible correspondence between the assertions we make about the world and the reality independent of us. When looking for patterns and formulating analysis, our claims have to cohere if we are to make sense of that reality, though we know that in the notoriously messy word of human affairs not everyone and everything fits a pattern that seems coherent. And we search for community agreement on values to govern our collective lives, recognizing that human nature sets the parameters in which we operate but that there have been many ways people have lived decent and meaningful lives within those parameters.

If this seems a rather superficial treatment of complex questions, that's because it is. Remember, my goal is not a treatise but scaffolding construction. From those basics, I want to move to two issues that have been the subject of reflection over millennia and are relevant to today's increasingly polarized debates. One is the tussling over the social construction of reality and the material constraints on those constructions. The other is the relationship between reason and emotion. These are questions about what we can trust ourselves to know about the world outside of us, and what we can trust ourselves to know about how we come to know.

BUILDING A PICTURE OF REALITY: CONSTRUCTED AND CONSTRAINED

The world exists independent of us, but what we can know about anything in that world comes through our experience. We construct an account of reality, and that account will reflect in some ways the linguistic, cultural, and political systems in which the account is constructed. It seems silly to ignore those shaping influences. But it also seems silly to assert that any account is plausible, and even sillier to imagine that all accounts are equally plausible. We construct, and at the same time we are constrained by material realities that we can't change.

Another way to say this: We can't construct *facts* that are contrary to material reality, at least not for long if we want to survive. But we are always constructing *knowledge claims*, assembling facts in the way we have reasons to believe is our best account of that material reality.

I use the term "material reality" to distinguish from "social reality," a realm in which humans construct things all the time out of whole cloth. A good example is marriage.

Anthropologists have observed that humans generally are a pair-bonding species. Most adults, though certainly not all, live with a mate, usually one at a time, though not necessarily for a lifetime. There are patterns in how humans create family structures. But the rules about those pair bonds—what constitutes a marriage, for example—change over time and from place to place. The pattern of pair-bonding is a material reality; the institution of marriage is socially constructed. The two are linked, but the material reality does not dictate a single set of rules for the social convention.

In the United States (and many other places), when a person who is authorized by the state to certify marriages—typically a clergy member, often a judge, maybe a county clerk—signs a certificate, two people who had been single are legally married, a social reality. Not so long ago, the signature usually came after "I now pronounce you man and wife." When feminists noted the sexism in the declaration, it shifted to "I now pronounce you husband and wife." In some parts of the world, that also could be "I now pronounce you wife and wife," or "husband and husband." Social realities change.

The human pair-bonding pattern is related to the social convention of marriage. If we weren't a pair-bonding species, it's hard to imagine the institution of marriage emerging. But being a pair-bonding species doesn't mean there is a single way that people create pair bonds.

Here are two hypotheticals to illustrate the difference between material and social realities, examples that are simple, but I hope not simplistic.

Imagine I assert that I have special access to divine wisdom and that if you approach me with the appropriate reverence, I will share that divine wisdom with you, which you can use to guide your life decisions. If I can persuade people of that—if I can make the case, and the case seems plausible in our culture, and there is no one or no institution blocking me—then I really do have special status. Some people will make choices based on what I say. A reality has been socially constructed, at least for the time being. I have become a person with the power to influence events because of what others accept as my special access to the category of the divine. That reality is socially constructed.

Now imagine that I assert I have an additional power in relation to the divine, which I claim gives me the ability to project significant amounts of electrical energy from my body to another person, at a level of intensity that could kill. No matter how many people might believe I have this power and act as if I might use it, I will never be able to pull it off. If I could get people in my community to believe this, I might be able to scare them, but I will never kill anyone with a jolt of electricity from my fingertips. That attempt at creating a new physical power—using words, invoking cultural beliefs, with some social power behind me—is constrained by material realities.

That may seem a bit silly, but it is a reminder to be precise in our use of the concept "the social construction of reality." Even the most extreme postmodern thinker would not worry that I could project an electrical charge through the use of language. Even people who believe in various kinds of supernatural forces aren't likely to quiver in front me if I were to threaten to send a deadly surge of current their way.

Let's go back to race and sex, the hot-button issues I'm focusing on. Here's the executive summary: Observable physical differences among people whose ancestors come from different continents are a material reality, but the concept of race is arbitrary and socially constructed. The sex binary of male/female is a material reality, but the gender binary of masculine/feminine is socially constructed. That presentation of material/social may suggest the two concepts are basically the same, but they are not. The differences matter.

On race: My ancestors come from northern Europe and Scandinavia. If I stand alongside a person whose ancestors come from Africa, the differences in such things as skin color, shape of noses, and hair texture are hard to miss. There are individual differences *within* groups of Europeans and *within* groups of Africans, and there are identifiable patterns in the differences in appearance *between* the groups. There also are patterns concerning such things as reactions to a specific drug or susceptibility to a specific disease depending on ancestors' region-of-origin. But scientists recognize that racial categories are poor proxies for genetic diversity.[51]

Human communities have always recognized in-group/out-group, but modern racial groupings have not always existed. One mark of their social construction is that we could eliminate racial categories and life could go on uninterrupted. After all, there are many observable differences in human beings—some of us have larger ears than others. That's a material reality just as much as differences in skin color. But we don't create politically/economically relevant categories around the size of our ears. We don't need to create categories around any of these superficial differences to organize a society.

What makes it so hard to let go of the concept of race is our racist history. White supremacy asserts that there are racialized differences that go beyond what can be observed, primarily differences in cognitive ability, moral reasoning, or emotional maturity. Those racialized claims were socially constructed to rationalize the brutality some whites used to increase their wealth and power through the exploitation of non-white groups. Many people still believe, overtly or covertly, in that white-supremacist claim. Others don't necessarily believe it but don't want to disturb the racialized distribution of wealth and power that benefits them. But if we were ever collectively to overcome our history and renounce the disparities in wealth and power, race could disappear.

On sex: Sex is a material reality, binary and biological. Male and female are marked by the kinds of gametes we produce, sperm or egg. Not every person born has the capacity to reproduce (there are anomalies) and not every person will reproduce (people make choices). But that does not change the fact that male humans can participate in reproduction only when their small gametes come together with the large gamete of a female human.

Gender is socially constructed, an insight from feminists who challenged patriarchal claims that men's domination and exploitation of women are natural because of biology. Only female humans bear children; that's a biological reality. Suggesting that because they bear children, women are not competent to participate in politics is a patriarchal gender norm. Patriarchy—the term for systems of institutionalized male dominance—turns biological difference into social dominance, enforced by rigid, repressive, and reactionary gender norms. Gender reflects the unequal distribution of power between men and women over the past few thousand years.

A test of whether something is socially constructed is whether it could be constructed differently. Race can be. Sex can't be. We could live just fine without the concept of racial differences. The species could not survive if we didn't recognize the concept of sexual differences.

So, race is constructed all the way down, even though we mark racial groups by observable physical difference. Gender is constructed out of sex differences that are central to reproduction, and hence, central to our lives and cannot be ignored. There can be a world without races but there cannot be a world without recognizing that there are two sexes that have different roles in reproduction. Gender is socially constructed on top of sex, sometimes in egalitarian ways (through most of human history) and sometimes in hierarchical ways (in the past few thousand years of patriarchy).[52]

People's reactions to these points vary widely, even within particular political projects.

Some reactionary conservatives hold onto a notion of white supremacy rooted in biology. Other conservatives reject that claim but offer only a limited critique of the inequities produced by white-supremacist systems. Some conservatives agree that biological sex is binary but reject a critique of patriarchy and believe that a rigid binary in cultural gender systems is appropriate. Religious conservatives often assert that such rigid norms are mandated by God.

Most people on the left side of the fence accept the social construction of race and ascribe inequities to white supremacy. But when it comes to sex/gender, people on the left vary widely, largely a result of the recent success of the ideology of the transgender movement, which I examine in Chapter 5.

This makes it important to digress for a moment to talk about science. A few years ago, I had a conversation with a feminist colleague with whom I was in political alignment on most things, except transgenderism. When she suggested that sex might not be binary and biological but a social construction itself, I said such a claim would require us to ignore what we know about human biology and reproduction from modern science as well as our everyday experience. Her response: "Well, science is just one story," implying we shouldn't take it as definitive. Well, yes, like any system of knowing, science does offer us an account of how the world works, which we could call a story. But does that mean we can reject it whenever it doesn't advance our preferred political position? How should we understand scientific stories?

MODERN SCIENCE AND ALTERNATIVES

Science, defined as the systematic study of phenomena of the natural world, is not just a collection of academic disciplines but a methodology. Modern science has created standardized methods for observation and experimentation, the results of which can yield accurate predictions when verified through repeated testing. Scientists use both inductive and deductive reasoning to form and test hypotheses and build theories. This approach to knowledge is, to date, the most powerful method we have for determining how the physical world works, from the subatomic to the galactic, for discerning what are sometimes called the "laws of nature."

A caution: That simple definition hides the rich and complex practices that make up the modern scientific enterprise. As Naomi Oreskes points out, there is no single scientific method but many methods that go forward under that general description, yet they all share a commitment to ensuring reliability by a rigorous vetting process.[53] But that doesn't mean scientists are always right or always agree, of course. Some people take disagreements among scientists to be a marker of failure, but Oreskes explains that is a sign of strength. Science is a social process that has rules that guide methods and collection of evidence, but also is enhanced by diversity of views. When people believe science got it wrong, it often involves cases in which there had been no consensus among scientists, where the process hadn't run its course.

Another caution: The more knowledge we accumulate, the more we realize what we don't know. That's why my friends Wes Jackson and Bill Vitek have long advocated an "ignorance-based worldview,"[54] not to celebrate stupidity but to emphasize that expanding knowledge should deepen our awareness of our even more expansive ignorance.

Here's a personal example of that: I took an introductory astronomy class in college and did well. Emboldened, I took the next-level astronomy class, which required a deeper understanding of the theory of relativity and related concepts—deeper, it turns out, than I was capable of at the time. I felt lucky to escape with a C. If I had gone further and taken a physics class in quantum mechanics, well, let's not speculate about the outcome. Knowing a little bit led me to greater understanding of the depths of my personal ignorance. That's true not only for individuals but for the culture. Expanding our collective knowledge should increase our awareness of what is unknown. But even with an appropriate level of humility, modern science has generated knowledge on a scale unprecedented in human history. Many of the questions we can now answer with some confidence couldn't have been formulated in even the recent past.

This success has not led to a uniform embrace of science as the primary way of knowing about the natural world. Most obviously, there have long been fundamentalist strains of various religions that reject any scientific claim that clashes with what is taken to be revealed truth. The most well-known example is some Christians' rejection of evolution by natural selection, whether that rejection is presented as a straightforward religious claim about divine creation or offered in the pseudo-scientific language of "intelligent design."[55]

But we should remember that literalism/fundamentalism is only one approach to religion. Because I grew up in a Christian culture, I'll stick to that faith tradition as an example. For my purposes here, the Christians I've met fall into one of three categories: those who believe in the supernatural claims of the Bible, those who don't, and those who avoid the question because it is so divisive.

By supernatural I mean those claims that cannot be understood as natural phenomena, most notably: the existence of God defined as an actual force, entity, or being with the power to direct activity in the world; a virgin birth; and the resurrection of Jesus. Some Christians believe those claims to be accurate accounts of history. Other Christians understand the faith as a historically contingent set of ideas about how to understand the larger world and how people should live, without endorsing supernatural claims. Those in this second group take stories about supernatural forces to be allegorical, mythical, poetic—sources of insight and wisdom that shouldn't be taken as factual accounts of history. Let's say, for the sake of discussion, that each group is about one-third of those who identify as Christian. The final third would be made up of folks who aren't sure and often resort to "We can't know" when asked to choose, hoping they can avoid the question.

Some, though certainly not all, of the Christians who embrace supernatural claims take issue with some of the knowledge generated by modern science, which generates irresolvable conflicts because of obvious differences in theories of knowledge—science does not recognize revealed truth. It's difficult to see how the conflicts can be resolved intellectually. As a result, policy disputes involving these conflicts tend to be settled not by intellectual engagement but in the political arena.

There also are secular skeptics, such as my colleague who tried to dismiss basic biology when discussing transgenderism. In my experience, these folks are usually ideologically committed activists and/or professional intellectuals, who embrace some version of faddish postmodern theory. Postmodernism, charitably defined, is the challenge to claims of certainty made by a variety of systems and philosophies of the modern period, the past five hundred years or so. It's good to challenge claims of certainty, so long as one doesn't deny that material realities exist independent of ideologies. We can, and should, study the social practices of scientists and the cultural/political/economic context of their work (that's the sociology of science or what is sometimes called science studies) and still recognize the power of the scientific method. One critic of my writing on transgenderism told me, "Biology is a colonial framework for fitting the world into a dichotomy," but I doubt that such jargon leads him to deny the insights of biology that are relevant to his daily life. In this sense, there is no real conflict except in occasional intellectual debates, which go on at a level of abstraction that tends not to affect people's policy preferences.

In short: Neither religion nor inflated academic rhetoric pose any serious challenge to modern science.

More interesting in recent years is the conversation about the relationship of science to indigenous traditions and premodern ways of knowing about the material world.[56] As the multiple cascading ecological crises intensify, an increasing number of people suggest that the dominant culture look to indigenous traditions as a guide. That can create tension with some scientists, but in this case that tension can be resolved by clarifying the differing levels of analysis each framework takes up.

Various terms have been used for this knowledge that comes from outside the practice of modern science: traditional knowledge (TK), indigenous knowledge (IK), or traditional ecological knowledge (TEK). For simplicity's sake, I will use TEK and MS (for modern science). Whatever the term, people from every part of the world have been accumulating knowledge about their places and how to live in them, and for too long Western science ignored or denigrated such knowledge.[57] Knowledge-seeking should go forward with mutual respect, but science has a colonial and imperialist history just like European political and economic institutions.[58] Precisely because of the multiple cascading ecological crises, it's imperative that we draw on all empirical ways of knowing about the larger living world.

I use the word "empirical" deliberately, to recognize that TEK and MS both are ways of observing and understanding natural phenomena. This is crucial to emphasize because some people assume that TEK is primarily rooted in spirituality or mythology, in part because indigenous methods of reporting knowledge don't always map onto the conventions of MS. In North America, for example, no pre-contact indigenous society had a written language as far as we know, which means knowledge was transmitted orally and often embedded in stories.[59] Discounting this knowledge is not only detrimental to indigenous people but to all of us; when any relevant knowledge that is integral to dealing with problems is excluded, everyone loses.

The success of various indigenous societies in using and safeguarding resources has required empirical knowledge built on keen observation in a particular geography, often built over long periods of time. In one of many examples, researchers have demonstrated that indigenous people in British Columbia, Canada, maintained clam gardens that likely increased productivity by altering the landscape and enhancing growing conditions for clams.[60] Such work depends on careful observation and understanding of organisms in ecosystems, whether that takes place within TEK or MS. As an archaeologist who studies postglacial North America puts it:

> As ways of knowing, Western and Indigenous Knowledge share several important and fundamental attributes. Both are constantly verified through repetition and verification, inference and

prediction, empirical observations and recognition of pattern events. ... Some types of Indigenous knowledge simply fall outside the realm of prior Western understanding. In contrast to Western knowledge, which tends to be text based, reductionist, hierarchical and dependent on categorization (putting things into categories), Indigenous science does not strive for a universal set of explanations but is particularistic in orientation and often contextual.[61]

Let me offer a personal example of these similarities and differences between TEK and MS. If I wanted to start growing food or feed crops for animals in the mountains of northern New Mexico where I currently live, I would be wise to pay attention to the practices of the indigenous population and the methods developed by those who colonized the region from Spanish Mexico, including the acequia system of flood irrigation that goes back centuries, to North Africa, Spain, and perhaps ancient Rome. I also might want to consider the advice from the state's farm service agents who have access to the latest agricultural research, although there's no guarantee that their advice would be more useful than that of my neighbors.

But if I want to learn about the geological formation of the Sangre de Cristo Mountains tens of millions of years ago, I won't look to TEK, precisely because its methods of observation and understanding in a specific location do not seek "a universal set of explanations" and cannot answer questions on that scale. TEK cannot tell us anything about plate tectonics, or such things as the nuclear fusion in the sun's core that is converting hydrogen into helium, generating the release of energy that travels to us. It's not that TEK is a lesser form of knowledge but rather knowledge with a different focus. Scientific principles that help us understand fundamental forces of the universe can't be generated from local observation.

Acknowledging this does not minimize the value of TEK in many situations nor does it devalue indigenous societies, but simply recognizes the different histories of different systems of generating knowledge. The botanist/ecologist Robin Wall Kimmerer, who is also an enrolled member of the Citizen Potawatomi Nation, is a leading voice for integration of ways of knowing. She writes:

> [TEK] is born of long intimacy and attentiveness to a homeland and
> can arise wherever people are materially and spiritually integrated
> with their landscape. TEK is rational and reliable knowledge that
> has been developed through generations of intimate contact by
> native peoples with their lands. TEK is being recognized as having
> equal status with scientific knowledge and has been termed the
> "intellectual twin to science." This long intellectual tradition exists
> in parallel to Western science, yet has been historically marginalized
> by the scientific community.[62]

My only quibble with that assessment is the terms "equal status" and
"intellectual twin," which obscure the different realms in which each
form of knowing has value. We should recognize the corrective that TEK
offers MS: "The indigenous ethos of a harmonious community of human
and non-human nature offers a necessary ecocentric corrective to the
anthropocentrism that has characterized so much of Western ecological
thought."[63] But that doesn't mean that TEK and MS offer the same kind
of knowledge.

Here's an analogy from my personal life. My wife, Eliza Gilkyson, and
I are both writers. We both have been writing for public audiences since
we were in high school. I started in journalism, moved into academic
writing, and now write essays and books. She is a songwriter and
performer in the folk music genre. Both our endeavors are called writing,
and because of our similar interests in the world we often write about
the same topics. But what she does is quite different from what I do. Do
we have equal status? We both respect and enjoy the other's work, but
I'm not sure what equal status would mean. If you want an argument for
the need to limit energy consumption, I would direct you to my writing
(Chapter 6 in this volume). If you want to wrestle with the emotional
realities of living in a culture in collapse, I would recommend her songs
(such as "The Great Correction," one of my favorites). Both my prose and
her poetry are a form of writing, creative in some ways, but distinctively
different. Our genres are perhaps cousins, but not intellectual twins.

Now, some cautionary notes. Modern science has generated
understandings of the world that no other system of knowing in human

history ever had the ability to produce. That's not to suggest the practice of MS is trouble free, especially today. Working scientists, both in and outside academic institutions, face intense demands to publish. As a result, the amount of research of questionable value has expanded. Peer review of research articles has become less reliable because of time constraints on everyone.[64] The influence of funders can create pressures, subtle and overt, to shape research results to their interests.[65] A leading medical researcher contends that "the way we pay for science does not encourage the best results."[66] Elitism and arrogance in the practice of science can lead ordinary people to mistrust the process. MS has more than its share of problems.

Nor can we celebrate everything that MS has produced or all the things modern scientists do. Mostly obviously, scientists created the knowledge that made nuclear weapons possible, one example of a longstanding connection between science and military applications of knowledge. Just as obvious is that without engineers' use of modern science to invent gadgets to burn coal and oil to do work, such as the steam engine and the internal combustion engine, we wouldn't be facing the current level of rapid climate disruption.

Perhaps more troubling than specific failures is the intertwined history of MS and human attempts to dominate the larger living world and treat all components of that world as resources available to humans. Francis Bacon, one of the founders of MS, articulated this goal in the context of Christian theology. The historian of science Carolyn Merchant explains that Bacon:

> forcefully proclaimed a secular program for the domination of nature and a pathway to recovering the paradise lost by Adam and Eve. Due to the Fall from the Garden of Eden, Bacon believed, the human race had lost its "dominion over creation." Bacon saw science and technology as the way to control nature and thereby to recover the right to the original garden given to the first parents.[67]

But the troubling origins of MS and the use of science for destructive purposes do not change the fact that our knowledge of the physical universe has expanded exponentially in the five centuries of the modern period of science. Perhaps we would be better off without these capacities, but that doesn't change how much we have come to know from that work.

Why are the limitations of both TEK and MS important to emphasize? Any approach to knowledge can answer some questions and not others, depending on its methods. It's crucial not to give in to temptations to overstate the capacity of human knowledge to deal with current crises, no matter where that knowledge comes from. Many questions about the nature of the universe are beyond any methods we currently can employ. It's helpful to remember that if we piled up all human knowledge to date, from every source, what we don't know would still far outstrip what we do know.

It can't be repeated too often: Humility on all sides is called for.

FEELING RATIONAL: REASON AND EMOTION

I was eight years old when the original *Star Trek* television series began in 1966. I don't recall when I first watched the show—it might not have been until after the show ended in 1969 and went into syndication. But I remember that my favorite character was Mr. Spock, perhaps a sign of my interest in the complexity of our internal experiences, though more likely an allegiance to the goofy-looking guy in a group.

To recap Spock's struggle: His Vulcan father came from a culture that used reason to eliminate emotion, an excess of which had been destructive, but he also inherited an emotional capacity from his human mother, creating inevitable tension.[68] The dual-planet heritage highlighted what all people face, what we call the internal battle of reason versus emotion. Should we do what's dictated by logic, or are our feelings a better guide?

Spock is a great character, even if the underlying premise—that reason and emotion are distinct and separate processes—isn't accurate.[69] But we shouldn't blame *Star Trek* for that, given how common the notion is. In the 1980s, faddish ideas about right and left brain—that creativity comes from the right and logical thinking from the left—entrenched the reason/emotion dichotomy further in pop psychology.[70] It's hard to escape, partly because our internal experience can sometimes feel like a reason-versus-emotion cage match. (At about the same time I was watching *Star Trek*, I also was watching professional wrestling.)

I never gave much thought to any of this until I was in graduate school and started reading philosophy. Two feminist philosophers challenged these simple dichotomies and expanded my horizons, and I've been quoting them ever since I first read their work.

We may talk about thinking and feeling as different processes, but they really are part of an organic, unified human engagement with the world that cannot be broken down into parts. Philosopher Sarah Hoagland explains why trying to separate them is counterproductive:

> Reasoning is not a substitute for emotions. Reasoning is part of the substance, direction, and perspective of emotions just as emotions are part of the texture, substance, and quality of reasoning. Trying to fragment them, even if at times it seems a relief or safer, or more intense, will only fragment our abilities. Trying to address only one is like trying to appreciate art by focusing only on one color. Creativity does not emerge when we fragment our selves.[71]

The other philosopher, Naomi Scheman, was a professor at the University of Minnesota, where I was in graduate school. I took her classes and talked her into serving on my dissertation committee. In an essay on anger, she challenges:

> the myth about the emotions, women's emotions in particular, that tells us they are irrational or non-rational storms. They sweep over us and are wholly personal, quite possibly hormonal. The emotions that fit with this picture tend to be diffuse, like moods, or episodic and undirected. They don't, in any event, *mean* anything. Thus we have outbursts of anger directed at children, the weather, or a piece of balky machinery. We often feel there's something not quite right about the anger; it's out of proportion, and, especially if aimed at children, feels unfair and wrong. Instead of encouraging us to interpret these outbursts, the myth makes us feel guilty for having succumbed.[72]

Why does any of this matter? One of the cheap ways people dismiss arguments by others is to suggest the person is overly emotional and incapable of dealing with a question rationally, especially when someone is angry. There certainly are times when our emotional reactions to events and people can overwhelm us and make it difficult, in that moment, to gather and evaluate evidence. The intensity of an emotion also can distort our perceptions of what is happening. We sometimes make bad judgments when we are angry.

But it's also true that an obsession with staying rational in the face of events that generate strong emotions can distort one's account of an event. Rejecting emotions as always nothing but irrational can be a way of avoiding what our emotions can tell us about reality. Getting angry when another person treats us unfairly can be important information as we evaluate the other person's actions.

In short: Emotions are not an argument, just as facts are not an argument. Arguments are built with facts, taking notice of our emotional reactions to the world.

Let's go back to the discussion of sexual assault. Violence and abuse can lead one to freeze, to be unable to act in the moment. One result of the trauma may be difficulty remembering the specific details of the event. That can make it hard for someone to present a clear account, which too often leads other people to assume the event may not have happened, or at least didn't happen in the way the victim believes. But that post-traumatic absence of clarity can also be understood as evidence of the intensity of the trauma. I'm not suggesting there's an easy way to establish with certainty what happened in such cases, but dismissing an account by tagging it as mere emotion is ill advised.[73]

Neuroscientist Vinod Goel suggests that instead of the dismissive term "irrational," we talk of the "arational," recognizing that there are noncognitive factors at work in our cognition. He offers the term "tethered rationality" to recognize that "both reasoning and nonreasoning systems are in play in human behavior. ... Humans have a reasoning mind, but it is tethered to and modulated by evolutionarily older associative, instinctive, and autonomic minds."[74] Two prominent psychologists—especially prominent because they served as consultants for the popular Pixar animated movie about emotions, *Inside Out*—reject the common idea that "emotions are enemies of rationality and disruptive of cooperative social relations," arguing that "emotions organize—rather than disrupt—rational thinking."[75]

Another psychologist, the author of the best-selling book *Thinking Fast and Slow*,[76] bluntly challenges the idea that reason dominates:

> Many ideas happen to us. We have intuition, we have feeling, we have emotion, all of that happens, we don't decide to do it. We don't control it. Then there are periods where we reason, where we think more slowly, more deliberately, and that's critical. We think we reason more than we actually do. There is a lot of what we think is thinking, is actually finding justifications and rationalizations for things, our fast thinking tells us what to do. So, it's that part that is really the dangerous part. We don't know our own minds.
>
> We think, each of us, that we're much more rational than we are. And we think that we make our decisions because we have good reasons to make them. Even when it's the other way around. We believe in the reasons, because we've already made the decision.[77]

If Daniel Kahneman is correct, then what's the point of all these reflections on how we think? Is reason simply a post-hoc rationalization for what we want, and want to believe, driven by internal forces we don't really control?

By now you can guess my answer: We don't know for sure. The safe bet is to develop our capacity to understand our emotional lives while we also develop our capacity to use reason to deepen our understanding of ourselves and the world.

Since I started this section with pop culture, I'll end with a science-fiction film, *The Matrix*, from a scene in which the messianic character Neo, still struggling with his revolutionary role, consults the Oracle. If the Oracle already knows what he will choose, Neo wonders how he can be acting freely. The Oracle dodges the free-will question and explains, "You didn't come here to make the choice. You've already made it. You're here to try to understand why you made it."

It's useful to think of ourselves as Neo, trying to understand our own behavior—and the behavior of others—with a mishmash of tools: logic, scientific research, the accumulated wisdom of various traditions, self-reflection about our emotional reactions. Pop culture can help, but we shouldn't lean too hard on it. After all, right after the Oracle offers that insight, she says, "We're all here to do what we're all here to do."

STRUGGLING TO THINK, TOGETHER

One assessment of the current cultural scene is that we are "post-truth," which was the Oxford Word of the Year in 2016. Here's the Oxford English Dictionary definition: "Relating to or denoting circumstances in which objective facts are less influential in shaping public opinion than appeals to emotion and personal belief."[78]

But if human decisions have always been the product of an unknowable interaction between reason and emotion, which are best thought of not as separate processes in the first place, then we've always been post-truth to some degree. That said, the conflicts over basic intellectual issues today—no matter how that compares with any past era—should concern us. This book is my contribution to trying to be uncertain in more productive ways.

Again, for emphasis: Our chances for increasing our productivity are enhanced if we remember that thinking is a social activity. We are often alone with our thoughts, but what we think is the product of a collective process. It's not just that no one of us can comprehend the vast store of knowledge accumulated by humans at this point, but that the common observation that we are social beings applies to our cognitive activity.

No one thinks alone, thank goodness. Even the most rigorous thinker is prone to biases that come from a desire to be correct, overriding the best evaluation of evidence possible. That's why we need each other, not just because my physicist friend knows a lot about quantum theory that I don't know, or that my dentist knows a lot more about teeth than I do. In all of our attempts to know the world, we all are on thin ice. It's a counterintuitive metaphor—we're on intellectual thin ice, and so we need to invite more people to join us. The added intellectual weight, spread across the whole lake, won't crack the ice but make our efforts stronger. OK, forget the thin-ice metaphor.

Philosopher Hrishikesh Joshi points out that "our epistemic health as individuals— i.e., the extent to which our beliefs accurately represent the world—is inextricably tied to the health of the epistemic commons."[79] (Remember, "epistemic" is a philosopher's term for our struggle to understand how we come to know things.) Joshi argues for an interactionist picture of our intellectual lives,[80] each of us with the capacity to contribute to the work required to get closer to *the* truth, not simply to our individual truths.

In the aptly titled book *The Enigma of Reason,* Hugo Mercier and Dan Sperber point out "two problems that plague laypeople in their solitary reasoning: myside bias and low evaluation criteria for one's own arguments—that is, laziness."[81] We want to find the evidence that supports what we already believe. In addition to "myside bias," this tendency goes by "confirmation bias," another type of motivated reasoning. And it's not just laypeople who fall into these traps, they point out, which is why they reject the solitary genius view of science.

In short, we're all in this together, whether we like it or not, whether we like each other or not.

That means we not only have a right to speak but an obligation to participate in the collective effort. If we don't, we are "free riders" in economics jargon—we use something produced by the efforts of others without contributing. When we fail to speak, especially about contentious issues, we may feel we are being sensitive to the needs of others who might not want to hear what we have to say. But, in fact, we are failing each other.

Let's keep that responsibility to speak in mind in the next chapter on freedom of speech.

Chapter 3:
Stepping Back: Speaking

I don't mean to be rude, but smart people sometimes say not-so-smart things about freedom of speech.

Let's start with Elon Musk, the boss at Tesla and SpaceX. I'm not interested here in Musk's head-scratching business decisions or his designed-to-annoy public comments, but instead in his often-quoted declaration that he is a "free-speech absolutist." After he bought Twitter (which he later renamed X) and then banished from the platform various people whose speech he didn't like, critics labeled Musk a hypocrite. I'm not much interested in that, either. I've never met anyone who didn't have a bit of hypocrisy hiding somewhere in their lives, myself included. A more important observation is that if Musk, and all the other people who claim to be free-speech absolutists, actually meant it, they would be admitting that they are moral monsters.

No one really means it. There is no such thing as a free-speech absolutist.[82]

To be a true absolutist—and to endorse that as the guiding principle for First Amendment law in the United States—would mean rejecting any limits on any speech no matter what the consequences. That's what "absolute" usually means—to do something, well, absolutely, without exceptions. Absolutism would mean there would be no libel laws allowing people to recover damages when others deliberately lie about them. There would be no laws against the distribution or possession of child sexual abuse materials, what was once more commonly called child pornography. There would be no laws against conspiring to murder someone. And the list goes on.

Imagine if I were to publish a story saying Elon Musk runs an international drug trafficking ring, that he uses those illicit profits to offset his hidden losses at Tesla, and that his mismanagement of the electric car company is the result of his addiction to fentanyl. That story is, to the best of my knowledge, false on all counts. If Musk sued me for knowingly making false and defamatory statements (the kind that injure one's reputation), he likely would recover money damages, punishing me for my speech, a rejection of an absolutist interpretation of freedom of speech. Most people would agree that libel law is justified.

If I were selling or buying child sexual abuse materials, which is illegal in every state and under US law, I doubt anyone would suggest my First Amendment rights have been violated. The production of these materials rightfully has been deemed to be inherently harmful to children. But even if I haven't produced it, the selling and buying of that material leads to increased production, and hence, increased harm to children. Most people would agree that should be prohibited—the connection between the production and consumption is clear.

If I lived next to a yappy dog and my neighbor refused to do anything to quiet the animal, most people would agree I do not have a right to kill my neighbor (or the dog). Imagine that I find another neighbor who is as annoyed as I am, and I provide that second neighbor with detailed information I've collected about when our yappy dog-owning neighbor will be alone at home and what window he will be sitting in front of, and I suggest a spot from which a clean shot can be taken, and my neighbor successfully hits the target. I would have participated in a conspiracy to commit murder, even though all I did was speak to my neighbor about a plan. Who endorses an absolutist interpretation of the First Amendment that gets me off the hook?

Here are some other forms of speech we punish without much concern about freedom of speech: perjury, true threats, inciting another to suicide, sexual harassment, insider trading, blackmail, fraud, unauthorized use of another's intellectual property. All of these acts can be accomplished through speech alone, but that doesn't mean we treat them as absolutely free speech.

The reason no one supports an absolutist application of freedom of speech is because speech can, and often does, cause harm. Lying about someone can damage their standing in a community, leading to loss of income and social connections. Selling and buying child sexual abuse materials increases the number of children abused by the producers. Planning with others to kill someone makes the planner as responsible for murder as the person who pulls the trigger.

Elon Musk is not the only person who makes the empty claim of being an absolutist. Nadine Strossen, a lawyer who served as president of the American Civil Liberties Union from 1991 to 2008, gave the prestigious Richard S. Salant Lecture on Freedom of the Press at the Harvard Kennedy School's Shorenstein Center on Media, Politics and Public Policy in 2015 (I include all those details to indicate this was a serious setting). In response to a question, she said:

> Well, I'm a free-speech absolutist. But, that doesn't mean that speech is always protected. Along with every other fundamental right, it may be restricted. And I'm going to use a lawyer's term here, if, but only if, you can show that the restriction promotes a countervailing goal of compelling importance that can't be promoted in any other way. And that's a very, and appropriately, hard burden of proof.[83]

So, Strossen is an absolutist who would not protect speech absolutely. I'm not taking issue with her articulation of a standard for restriction but with her incoherent use of "absolutist." It reminds me of a friend who told me that she was a vegetarian. I said I didn't realize she had stopped eating meat. She said, "Well, I eat a little chicken and fish." I said, "Well, then you're not a vegetarian." She was annoyed with me, apparently wanting to claim the label without having to adhere to its common definition. Using "absolutist" to describe a First Amendment interpretation that isn't absolutist seems to be a similar rhetorical trick, in this case claiming a political purity that doesn't exist.

What "absolutist" appears to mean, as Strossen suggests, is something like this: "I will impose a high standard in evaluating any restriction on speech. In complex cases where there are conflicts concerning competing values, I will default to the most expansive space possible for speech that is consistent with other people's rights and safety." That's a perfectly defensible statement, but it's absolutist in the same sense as my chicken-and-fish-eating friend was a vegetarian.

No matter how obvious the problem of claiming absolutism, it continues to be used, not only by quirky CEOs and political activists but also by reputable law professors writing in reputable law journals:

> For roughly half a century, First Amendment doctrine has provided Americans with exceptionally broad protection for freedom of expression. To a degree that is unusual around the world, even among other constitutional democracies, American constitutional law generally protects expression of even the most hateful, offensive, illiberal, and dangerous ideas. This First Amendment absolutism, moreover, has been a striking point of judicial consensus, even on our current, badly fractured Supreme Court.[84]

Here's another description from a recent scholarly book: "The most unyielding analysis of the First Amendment is the absolutist approach, which views the First Amendment proscriptions as inflexible: Congress shall make no law, period."[85] No law means no law, except when it doesn't. And it has never meant no law, because it can't mean no law.

Those who endorse this kind-of/sort-of/not-really absolutism often come from a libertarian political position, on either the right or left side of the political fence, that prioritizes individual liberty over other social concerns. For example, in the debate about whether racist hate speech should be punished, libertarians typically reject any constraints on people's right to use racist slurs, even though they might reject the use of such slurs themselves. Supporters of hate-speech regulation suggest that in certain situations, free-speech concerns should be subordinated to the goal of eradicating racism and protecting the targets of that racist speech. This assertion of a priority for collective equality over individual liberty is almost exclusively articulated on the left, though not all liberal/progressive/left people agree.

What position is most consistent with the First Amendment to the US Constitution, and more generally, free-speech principles? Whatever one's view, an invocation of absolutism cannot answer the question.

Time for a brief note on terminology. I've been using the phrase "freedom of speech" so far. The First Amendment states that "Congress shall make no law ... abridging the freedom of speech, or of the press." There is a longstanding debate about whether those terms cover expression that is not conveyed by traditional notions of speaking or publishing, referred to as "symbolic speech" (burning a flag is one example). I won't address symbolic speech in this book, but I will start using the phrase "freedom of expression" as the most expansive description of these activities.

BEYOND ABSOLUTISM: SPEECH'S VALUE AND HARM

If not absolutism, how should we approach these issues? Let's start with recognition of two universal characteristics of *Homo sapiens*: We are a meaning-making and storytelling species. It's hard to imagine a human community in which people don't try to make sense of the world around them and then tell each other stories about what it means. The paleoanthropologist Ian Tattersall puts it this way:

> [F]or all the infinite cultural variety that has marked the long road of human experience, if there is one single thing that above all else unites all human beings today, it is our symbolic capacity: our common ability to organize the world around us into a vocabulary of mental representations that we can recombine in our minds, in an endless variety of new ways.[86]

Here's another universal: Every society draws a line between the stories one can tell freely, without the risk of punishment, and the stories that might get you in trouble. The line will be different from society to society, and different in a single society over time. But every society distinguishes between permitted and prohibited speech.

Once we jettison simplistic notions about absolutism and accept the inevitability of line drawing, we can get down to the business of balancing. In deciding where to draw the line, we are balancing the *value* of the expression against the *harm or potential harm* that expression can cause.

Go back to the examples above. Speaking with others to plan a murder is speech that has no social value and can result in the ultimate harm. Almost everyone would agree that child sex abuse material is extremely low-value speech (of value, I suppose, only to those who become sexually aroused by the sexual exploitation of children) and cannot be created without extraordinary harm. Assessing how false assertions of fact may injure someone's reputation gets more complicated, which is reflected in the complexity of libel law. How do we determine the truth about complex accusations when there is conflicting evidence? How do we make sure politicians and other powerful people don't use the threat of libel lawsuits to silence critics? But almost everyone accepts the need for some kind of legal recourse for those who are defamed, because lies about others have no value and the harm to reputation can have devastating consequences.

Sometimes these value/harms assessments are easy. More often they are not, and so become the subject of serious debate. Let's first take up differing assessments of the value of different kinds of expression, and then the question of how to understand harm and how to assess the consequences of expression that harms.

Some libertarians want to settle the question of the value of speech by avoiding it altogether, by asserting that we should not distinguish between types of expression, that a collective determination that some types of speech have greater value is inherently authoritarian. In this balancing act, a well-reasoned philosophical treatise on the nature of democracy has the same status as a cigarette advertisement, which strikes a lot of people (including me) as absurd.[87]

To start wrestling with the differing value we place on different types of speech, we can think about the reasons we want to protect speech in the first place. What are the potential justifications for freedom of expression? Once again, I'll summarize a rich literature on the subject with a list of three: political, psychological, and philosophical. (Intellectual is really the more accurate term, but it doesn't start with a P and I've already confessed my affection for alliteration.)

- Political: If we want a government that is as democratic as possible, freedom of expression is essential. If leaders can easily constrain the way citizens communicate about politics, then citizens cannot discuss political ideas and policy options, which makes meaningful participation in the process impossible. "Government of the people, by the people, for the people" requires the free flow of information and opinion.

- Psychological: The ability to express oneself is necessary to being one of those meaning-making/storytelling humans. It's impossible to become a fully self-realized person—someone with self-awareness and insight—without freedom of expression. Constrain our ability to express ourselves too much, and we feel incomplete. A key part of this is artistic expression, not just of professional artists but of everyone, since we all are capable of creativity.

- Philosophical/intellectual: Our inquiry into what the world is and how it works, as I've argued already, is social, requiring communication between inquirers. Without the freedom to explore ideas, truth-seeking would be hobbled. If a society's received wisdom is false, how can it be corrected without freedom of expression? Shutting down freedom of expression inevitably leads to the entrenchment of stifling dogma. As John Stuart Mill pointed out in the nineteenth century, even if that received wisdom is true, "If it is not fully, frequently, and fearlessly discussed, it will be held as a dead dogma, not a living truth."[88] (More on Mill's arguments in the Conclusion.)

Without meaningful guarantees of freedom of expression, people would be constrained in their attempts to participate in self-governance, to develop themselves to the fullest extent possible, and to come to deeper understandings of reality.

If we stopped there, a truly absolutist view of freedom of expression might make some sense. But there's the issue of harm. Let's go back to the classic concern that free speech shouldn't protect someone "falsely shouting fire in a theatre and causing a panic." If someone did that, no matter whether as a juvenile prank or a malicious attempt to injure, the balancing is easy—the speech has no social value and could potentially lead to people dying. We draw the line in a way that does not protect such expression.

But the case in which that example was used, *Schenck v. United States*,[89] concerned legitimate dissent, not a false statement that would cause a dangerous stampede. The socialists who were convicted under the Espionage Act of 1917 had not called for violence but argued that the draft for World War I violated the Thirteenth Amendment prohibition against involuntary servitude. Yet a fear of political violence sparked by speech is sometimes reasonable. It's not hard to imagine, especially on the heels of the January 6, 2021, attack on the US Capitol, that the persuasively expressed rejection of existing governmental authority can incite people to commit violence. Sometimes that violence may be justifiable (after all, I'm writing in a country that celebrates its founders' willingness to use violence to overthrow the legally constituted government of the time to create the United States of America). Sometimes that violence may be impossible to justify (January 6 is a good example). Whether justifiable or not, there's no doubt that rhetoric can be the if-not-but-for element of an outbreak of violence—that is, the violence would not have happened if not but for the speech.

Remember that we are talking here about political speech, which has high value. So, when would agents of the US government—remembering that "government," at least in theory, means representatives of the people—be justified in shutting down a speaker to prevent violence? The US Supreme Court's answer is that such suppression is justified when the speech is "directed to inciting or producing imminent lawless action" and is "likely to incite or produce such action."[90] But whatever standard one deems appropriate, we should acknowledge that the potential harm is serious and can't be dismissed by invoking a nonsensical claim to absolutism.

HARMS OF HARASSMENT

Let's take another complicated example, sexual harassment, defined as "unwelcome sexual advances, requests for sexual favors, and other verbal or physical harassment of a sexual nature."[91] Here's more legal language: "Quid pro quo" harassment (from Latin, "something for something") happens when "submission to or rejection of such conduct by an individual is used as the basis for employment decisions affecting such individual." In other words, if you reject a sexual advance from your boss, you will be fired. "Hostile environment" cases need not include a direct request for sexual activity.[92] In those situations, the conditions might be so miserable that a person decides to quit. In some cases, the misery might be the result of speech alone, of things a supervisor or coworker said to an employee.

In this case we are dealing with low-value speech—no one argues that democracy, self-realization, or truth-seeking are at stake in harassing speech. But what one person experiences as harassment could be defended by the speaker—and often is—as a joke or as acceptable social interaction, speech with some value. And how do we decide when harm has been done? Here is the federal government's guidance for cases in schools:

> In order to give rise to a complaint under Title IX, sexual harassment must be sufficiently severe, persistent, or pervasive that it adversely affects a student's education or creates a hostile or abusive educational environment. For a one-time incident to rise to the level of harassment, it must be severe."[93]

Obviously, any two people might disagree on what constitutes "severe, persistent, or pervasive." That's always the nature of the law—it is articulated in language not mathematical formulas, and even words with relatively clear meaning in the abstract can be the subject of dispute when used to describe actions in the world. The law says we should judge these things using a reasonable-person standard—what "a reasonable person would consider intimidating, hostile, or abusive."

But what is reasonable in a world in which, as I pointed out in Chapter 2, men's sexual violence and exploitation of women is so routine? If a woman has experienced multiple sexual assaults, is her judgment of what is reasonable likely to be the same as a man who has never had such an experience?[94] Should the standard be explicitly pegged to the experiences of girls and women? Should we use a "reasonable woman" standard? For that woman, a single incident of harassment may not meet the severe/persistent/pervasive standard but may be devastating and lead her never to return to a job or classroom. And since boys and men can also be sexually harassed, and some of them may have experiences of past abuse, should the standard be the most vulnerable people in society?

Whatever standard and reference we adopt, in some cases the harm of this psychological distress may not be readily evident to an outside observer. But psychological harm is clearly harm, even when people are really good at hiding it, which tends only to add to distress. It may be easier to see that someone has a broken leg than chronic depression, but both are real sources of pain.

So far, I've focused on the harm to the individuals targeted. But sexual harassment also shores up patriarchy and male dominance— harm at the collective level as well. When a male employer or teacher sexually harasses a female employee or student, the social message is: *Women and girls are for male pleasure, and there is nothing you can do about it.* When institutions do little to protect those harassed, the message is that harassers are more important. Even if the harasser is female, the message remains corrosive: People with power can do as they please to people without power.

The same observations apply to racial harassment, defined as the use of "racial slurs, offensive or derogatory remarks about a person's race or color, or the display of racially offensive symbols."[95] Individuals' previous experiences of racist abuse and attacks will no doubt affect their interpretation of a racist remark at work or school. Reasonable people will not all react the same way, and a reasonable-person standard leaves more vulnerable people unprotected. And racist expression affects not only the individual who is targeted but reinforces a white-supremacist system.

This abbreviated exploration of the harms of sexual and racial harassment isn't meant to resolve how we should write laws and policies.

Rather it reminds us that there are no simple or straightforward ways to resolve this balancing of the value of speech against its harm or potential harm. That means there are no simple or straightforward ways to adjudicate disputes about freedom of expression, either in court or in public.

THINKING AND SPEAKING FOR OURSELVES

We think together but we can also think for ourselves. Intellectual work is a social endeavor, and collectively we have to draw lines about freedom of expression. But to live authentically, we also have to think and speak by ourselves and for ourselves. We are herd animals, but no one wants to turn over all decision-making to the herd.

So, we all come up with our own rules for thinking, speaking, and acting. I don't believe that my approach to intellectual life and freedom of speech is particularly controversial, but I will present the rules I try to live by, using "I-statements." (That was a small joke, referencing the common admonition from psychotherapists not to blame others but to speak about one's own experience.)

- I will advocate for a position only after responsible study and evaluation to construct, to the best of my ability, a compelling analysis of reality.
- I know that my analysis could be wrong, because all human knowledge-seeking in a complex world is incomplete and fallible.
- I will adopt a different analysis when it's demonstrated that my arguments are unsound or that another analysis offers a better account of reality, based on mutually intelligible reasons.
- I will not adopt a different analysis simply because of legal requirements, institutional demands, or peer pressure, and will do my best to resist official or informal coercion.
- I will speak publicly about the conclusions I reach when I believe I can contribute to the collective process of understanding the world.

Those five rules seem simple but can be hard to put into practice.

In the following chapters, I want to move beyond philosophical and legal issues to engage with some of the most divisive debates that have emerged in the past decade, first about a critique of white supremacy (a critique that I think is a good thing) and second about transgender ideology (an ideology that I think has had dangerous consequences). Then I will tackle the thorniest problem our species faces, those multiple cascading ecological crises and the widespread denial of the need for limits.

Chapter 4:
Defining Racism: Individual Bigotry and Beyond

I am not an expert on race, but I have played one on TV. Here's my story.

As I noted in Chapter 1, in 1998 I published an article explaining the concept of white privilege[96] that circulated widely online, just as email was becoming common and it was relatively easy to cut and paste text from the web. There were many people more qualified than I to discuss the issues, but that fluke exposure led to more writing,[97] eventually a book, media appearances, and invitations to speak. While I was getting ready to leave for those speaking engagements, one of my friends would mockingly say I was going out to perform as "Robert Jensen, race expert."

The mockery was appropriate, and it always reminded me to preface my lectures with a statement that my area of scholarly expertise was not race and ethnicity, and that my experience in the world was one of unearned advantages that come with being white. What I know about the subject has come from cross-racial organizing efforts and from reading, mostly the work of non-white people, which I hope has helped me develop a critical eye for how race plays out in everyday life.

When I made presentations on *The Heart of Whiteness*,[98] I would start by saying, "I can guarantee you there is not a single original idea in this book." That was my way of saying I realized that most everything that needed to be said about race had been said, especially by writers of color. I often described the book as "warmed-over James Baldwin," acknowledging how much I had learned from the perceptive essays he had written as far back as the early 1960s about how white supremacy warped white people's consciousness.[99] I also pointed out the irony of being invited to speak: Because of white supremacy there were many occasions in which white people would be more likely to listen to the message when it came from another white person.

With all that acknowledged, I think I have something to contribute to the conversation and debate about, to use the subtitle of my book, "race, racism, and white privilege," though I have pretty much stopped using the latter phrase. Like so many terms that emerge to describe a real phenomenon—in this case, the unearned advantages that come to white people in a white-supremacist society—"white privilege" has in some circles become a punching bag or a punch line, distorted and caricatured by opponents and used too often by proponents without a clear definition.

My goals in this chapter are 1) to offer a framework for thinking about race, racism, and white supremacy, which will be a direct challenge to those who want to avoid reckoning with that system; and 2) to offer some conceptual clarity to those who want to face these issues honestly. That's no small task, given the hair-trigger nature of the current conversation about race.

WHERE ARE YOU FROM?

Here's an example of that tension: Asking a person "Where are you from?" can be troublesome. That seems like an innocent question, except when it is weighed down by centuries of white supremacy. So, let's start with an example that reminds white people to be careful about claiming innocence.

In most cases, the question is routine in human interaction. I was born and raised in North Dakota. When I run into another North Dakotan and ask "Where are you from?" I just want to know the person's hometown. (For those interested, I was born in Devils Lake and grew up mainly in Fargo, the biggest city in the state, the first city in North Dakota to get a McDonald's, in 1969.)

But imagine a more complex situation. Someone who looks like me (white, with European ancestors) meets someone whose appearance and/or name suggests ancestors from South Asia. In that case, "Where are you from?" could mean at least two different things: 1) I would like to know more about you, in part because we seem to have roots in different parts of the world. Can you tell me about yourself and what you and your family consider home? Or 2) I see that you are different from me. You aren't one of us. Who are you and why are you in my space?

The first version is not only the result of normal curiosity but an indication that I want to learn about other cultures in this multicultural society. The second is a challenge to a person's political and cultural standing. Remember that in the United States, citizenship is not a function of race or ethnicity. Being an American is about your standing in a political community. A question that challenges that standing based on presumed racial or ethnic identity suggests that "real" Americans are white (or also possibly other race/ethnicity categories, depending on the person asking) but not South Asian.

The trick is how to convey the first meaning without accidentally implying the second.

I talked to hundreds of students in the years I taught at the University of Texas at Austin, including many from Asia or of Asian heritage. Typically, their names or physical features made it clear they didn't fit in the three largest racial/ethnic groups in Texas: white, black, and Hispanic.

I liked learning about students' backgrounds, not only so I could understand them better but also to expand my knowledge of the world. To avoid anyone interpreting my questions as a challenge to their right to be at the university, I developed various ways of asking about their roots. My go-to question for all undergraduates, no matter what their race or ethnicity, was, "Where did you go to high school?" Sometimes a student who had a South Asian name was an immigrant, but more often they were from Houston or Dallas (sometimes it felt like almost all my students were from either Houston or Dallas). After that, I would ask students—again, no matter what their identity—"Are your parents from Texas?" Sometimes the answer was no, that mom and dad had immigrated from India or Pakistan (less frequently from Bangladesh, Bhutan, Nepal, or Sri Lanka). That allowed me to ask about their experience. "Have you traveled there?" Many had, usually to visit family. I would ask what part of the country they visited. If they said Chennai in India, for example, I would ask if they spoke Tamil, the first language of that city, or Hindi, the national language. If they said Lahore in Pakistan, I would ask about Punjabi and Urdu. If I didn't recognize the city, I would ask for a quick geography lesson. These questions would often lead to a conversation about growing up in Texas as both a fairly typical suburban shopping mall-based teenager and someone who understood South Asian traditions.

I inquired only so long as the student seemed engaged. In my experience, most students were eager to talk about their lives and families. White students from West Texas were as eager as immigrant students. I learned a lot from these conversations, as did the students. If I had been afraid of offending students and avoided the subject of heritage, I would have missed out on interesting conversations and the students would have missed the chance to talk about important aspects of their lives.

On the other hand, when someone presses the "Where are you from?" question in a way that is insulting or abusive, we should hold them accountable. A recent example in the news as I was writing this book involved a white staff member of the royal family in the United Kingdom, who badgered Ngozi Fulani with the question after the black woman had said she was born and raised in the UK. Susan Hussey pressed: "No, but where do you really come from, where do your people come from?" which led Fulani to state, "I am of African heritage, Caribbean descent, and British nationality."[100] (Her parents immigrated from Barbados in the 1950s, part of what is called the "Windrush generation" that came from the Caribbean and faced racial discrimination.) After negative publicity about the exchange, Hussey apologized and resigned. No doubt some white Brits shrugged it off, saying Hussey was clumsy but meant no harm. But Fulani explained that the question left her having to try to read a white person's motivations. Not only did she feel the need to challenge Hussey, but she also had to deal with the fear that she would be blamed if she did, and that as a result the nonprofit group she leads would be hurt. "As a black person,

I found myself in this place where I wanted to say something but what happened would automatically be seen as my fault, it would bring [my charity] Sistah Space down," she said.[101]

DEFINITIONS

I offer those thoughts on "Where are you from?" not because it's the most pressing concern in the pursuit of racial justice but to remind us that everyday interaction is fraught with potential for insult and injury. I want to renew my insistence on clear definitions, not because that will eliminate such tensions, but so that difficult conversations aren't more difficult than necessary because of miscommunication. One example of how that happens comes when two people have fundamentally different definitions of racism.

Let's go back to the royal staff member, whose comment reflected a subtle white-defined view of the UK—"real" Brits are white, and Brits who aren't white really belong to some other place and are something less than fully British. I don't know what thoughts went through Susan Hussey's mind after the incident, but I wouldn't be surprised if she had thought to herself, "I'm not racist," which is a pretty common response from white people who are challenged. That statement usually is intended to mean something like, "I am not prejudiced against people who aren't white and therefore things I said could not have been racist." That definition of racism is focused on individuals and their accounts of their own intentions. Other definitions focus on unconscious assumptions and institutional realities.

Some may argue that too much time spent on seemingly academic issues around definitions is a diversion and that at this point in history there should be no confusion. But in my experience, the expanded public space for conversation about racial justice in recent years has not always led to greater clarity in how we use words. For example, the terms "systemic," "structural," and "institutional" racism are often tossed into conversations without a commonly understood definition, which undermines effective communication. There is not one correct meaning of such terms, and if there should be, I am not arrogant enough to think

I can prescribe those definitions. But in this chapter, I offer a framework that helps me understand complex problems and sort through potential solutions.

WHITE SUPREMACY AND RACISM

Before addressing systemic, structural, and institutional racism, we should define racism itself. That starts with white supremacy, the social/political system that developed in Europe about five hundred years ago. White supremacy was not the primary motive for the European conquest of much of the rest of the globe (that was mostly old-fashioned greed, self-aggrandizement, and grandiose thinking), but a doctrine of white/European/Christian supremacy evolved as a justification for conquest and hardened into dogma.

Eventually that doctrine took root in places where Europe established settler colonies, including the United States and South Africa, perhaps the two most deeply racist societies of the twentieth century outside of Nazi Germany. European barbarism was not the first instance of one group of people exterminating or exploiting others—that's been going on since the beginning of what we call, ironically, civilization—but it is the beginning of the modern conception of racism. White supremacy established the racial hierarchy that we live with today, with that one racial group's domination asserted to be the "natural" order of things.

To put it simply: racism is an embrace of the idea of racial hierarchy, generated by an ideology of white supremacy, which can be expressed both by individuals and through the practices of institutions.

That helps us sort out a vexing question: *Who can be racist in the United States?* Is racism any prejudice based on racial differences? Under that definition, a black person who doesn't want to associate with white people and whites who don't want to associate with blacks are all racists. Racial-justice advocates usually reject that, defining racism as "prejudice plus power," which means people of color can't be racist given their lack of collective power in a white-supremacist society.

But power is not a simple commodity that one group has exclusively and other groups lack completely. Imagine a successful black business owner with a Harvard degree passing a white homeless person who dropped out of high school and is panhandling on the street. If they exchanged racialized insults, whom do we label a racist? Who has power in that moment? What if the business owner is an immigrant from Vietnam and the panhandler is black? Is a white person's opposition to affirmative action programs evidence of racism? Does that assessment change if Chinese Americans oppose such programs?

Rather than searching for a one-size-fits-all-situations answer, we can say that the modern idea of racial hierarchies, with northern Europeans at the top, is the product of five hundred years of white supremacy. Absent white supremacy, those questions wouldn't be asked in this fashion. Again, that doesn't mean people always lived in peace and harmony before European imperialism and colonialism. History offers many versions of domination and subordination, justified in many different ways. But the concept of race we live with today emerges out of white supremacy.

White supremacy is not static, of course. As many scholars have pointed out, some people we now classify as white—including Italians, Irish, Slavs, Catholic Germans—weren't considered to be white when they first immigrated to the United States.[102] Demographic trends indicate that sometime in this century the United States will become a "majority-minority" country, with non-Hispanic whites making up less than half the population. In one of my first media appearances as a "race expert"—a panel discussion for a Black Entertainment Television talk show, sometime around 2000—sociologist Andrew Hacker wryly said that Hispanic people were seen by some white people as "whites in training," available to be mobilized into the category of white when the decline in the European-American population threatens whites' majority status. One contemporary scholar uses the term "multiracial whiteness" to describe the Trump-era Republican Party's pitch to people of other races and ethnicities that they can benefit from white privilege by supporting the GOP. She writes:

> Multiracial whiteness promises Latino Trump supporters freedom from the politics of diversity and recognition. For voters who see the very act of acknowledging one's racial identity as

itself racist, the politics of multiracial whiteness reinforces their desired approach to colorblind individualism. In the politics of multiracial whiteness, anyone can join the MAGA movement and engage in the wild freedom of unbridled rage and conspiracy theories.[103]

Laws and living conditions change, but the idea of racial hierarchies remains potent, and not only in the white community. When a non-white person from one racial group uses a racist slur against someone from a different non-white group, white supremacy is strengthened. For example, the anti-black racism in various Hispanic communities[104] doesn't prove that "everyone deep down is racist," but rather demonstrates the power of white supremacy to pull anyone into accepting hierarchical social arrangements.

That provides a framework for proceeding to examine racism at two different social levels (individual and institutional) with two different levels of awareness (overt and unconscious). In all these cases, we'll see that racism is both an idea and a set of practices.

INDIVIDUALS' OVERT RACISM

People who say, "I believe white people are smarter than [fill in the blank]," or "White people should run the world," are white supremacists. That's not controversial, but such statements are not all that common these days, even from people who otherwise sound a lot like white supremacists. For example, the Proud Boys, which many of us consider to be an overtly racist group, is sometimes described as "a white supremacist-adjacent organization"[105] because most of its members avoid blatant expressions of racism, at least in public. One of its most prominent members, Enrique Tarrio, is of Afro-Cuban descent.[106]

What should we call people who belong to groups that do not embrace unequivocally racist statements but instead advocate "white pride" or "Western chauvinism"? What about a politician who denies being racist but who denounces critical race theory and mischaracterizes that analysis as being rooted in antipathy toward whites and a desire to make white people feel miserable? Is it accurate to describe any of these people as overt racists?

Whether or not such folks think of themselves as holding racist ideas, they are supporting racist politics. The practical outcome of their position is to shore up white supremacy, whether they agree with that assessment of their rhetoric and actions or not. This smacks of telling people that they don't understand themselves, that they have motivations for their politics different than they claim. But being unaware of what our words and deeds reveal about ourselves is not unique to white supremacists—a lack of complete self-awareness is a feature of being human. We are all influenced by forces we may not fully understand, which means we don't always know ourselves very well.

INDIVIDUALS' UNCONSCIOUS RACISM

All of us who grew up in the United States were socialized in a white-supremacist society and influenced to varying degrees by that training. Through conscious efforts, we can minimize the effects of that training, but it is the rare white person who has transcended white supremacy. We should try to self-monitor as much as possible and stay open to critiques of our behavior from others. But self-monitoring is hardly foolproof, given how easily humans can self-deceive, and avoiding critique from others is easy, especially if we live relatively segregated lives.

That means when white people begin a sentence with "I'm not a racist, but ...,"[107] the smart bet is that the next thing out of their mouth will be a racist comment. The phrase suggests that a person lacks a well-developed capacity for critical self-reflection about that socialization. Most white people struggling to be antiracist have learned not to use that phrase. In fact, to demonstrate how seriously antiracist they are, some white people will go the other direction, prefacing a comment with "I know I'm a racist, but ...."[108] That phrase is no doubt well intentioned, signaling an awareness of that socialization, but it is debilitating. If every white person—including those actively engaged in antiracist education and organizing—is a racist, then the term is simply a synonym for being white. If the leader of the local neo-Nazi group is a racist and I'm a racist, then the term lacks useful meaning.

Failing to distinguish between actively racist and struggling-to-be-antiracist white people matters. Imagine going to white people and saying, "We want you to commit to personal and political action to challenge racism, which includes critical self-reflection about how you have internalized white supremacy, but no matter how hard you work at that, you're still a racist and always will be." That's a stunted view of human capacities for intellectual growth and moral reflection, and not exactly a great way to encourage people to embrace a movement for racial justice.

INSTITUTIONAL: SYSTEMIC RACISM

One common response to the messiness over adjudicating whether individuals' words and deeds are racist is to focus on institutions. Rather than argue about who is and isn't a racist, we can focus on what happens when people come together in groups. That's important, though we also interact daily as individuals, trying to understand one another, and so the macroanalysis doesn't eliminate questions about individuals and their motivations.

But it's true that treating racism as nothing more than individual attitudes and behavior is inadequate for political change. The most common terms for this collective focus are institutional, systemic, and structural racism. I have never found widely agreed upon definitions of the terms, and sometimes they are used interchangeably. I want to suggest distinctions that might be analytically useful.

Social movements have brought significant changes—some legal, some cultural—that have greatly reduced the frequency of racist expressions and behaviors in the United States. But racist patterns persist. Systemic racism suggests that today's racist outcomes are not the product of the proverbial "few bad apples" but rather of how certain systems operate.

An example is the disproportionately high rates of disciplining black students in the US public school system,[109] the result at least in part of black children being mistakenly judged as angry more often than white children.[110] The staffs of the nation's schools are disproportionately white,[111] but there's no reason to believe that white teachers are more racist than the white population.[112] It's likely that widely held assumptions (either overt or unconscious) and routine practices (either authorized or informal) result in a pattern of teachers referring students for disciplinary action differently based on race.

The problem we're focused on here is not the criteria for discipline or how classrooms are organized, which one may want to change for other reasons, but in how those criteria are applied. In such a system, it would be possible to change racist outcomes by retraining existing personnel or replacing those who resist with antiracist staff, and hiring more teachers of color. Racism is systemic, in the sense of being present throughout the system, but not necessarily a permanent feature of the system. We can imagine the same system producing fewer and less intense racist outcomes with modifications. In the face of systemic racism, individuals' actions can make a significant difference when people work together to change the routines and challenge racist attitudes and behaviors.

INSTITUTIONAL: STRUCTURAL RACISM

I suggest we use the term structural racism for systems in which white supremacy is more "baked in," making a more fundamental change in structure necessary. Again, schools provide a good example.

In the United States, public education is funded partly through local property taxes. That means wealthier school districts can raise more money for education than poorer districts.[113] That may be in general unfair, but it becomes structurally racist when we take into consideration two other facts: there is a racialized wealth gap,[114] especially between white and black/brown communities, and the United States is still overwhelmingly segregated in housing.[115] The result is that black and brown children will, on average compared with white children, attend schools with fewer financial resources. Those students will go to schools with less experienced teachers, fewer technological resources, older textbooks, fewer enrichment programs, and school facilities that are not as well maintained. Those non-white children, on average, will not get an education equal to white children.[116]

Public education is unequal in resource allocation, not simply because of individual attitudes and behaviors, but because of larger choices made long ago about structuring school funding,[117] making it a kind of structural racism. Dedicated teachers working in such a system can lessen the effects of the funding disparities, but on average black and brown children will not get the same quality of education as white children.

That leaves the term "institutional racism," which could be a synonym for either systemic or structural racism, and people seem to use it both ways. In previous writing, I used it to mean structural racism, but today I lean toward using it as an umbrella term for both the systemic and structural. Again, there's not a single right way to define these terms. The goal is shared understanding to improve communication, sharpen analysis, and guide policy.

DEFINITIONS SHAPE POLICY OPTIONS

Clear definitions help us evaluate policy options. In our school examples, when the problem is systemic racism, there are certain remedies to pursue, mostly focused on improving or changing personnel, or instituting a review system so that racist patterns in decisions can be identified and reversed. That's not easy but doesn't necessarily require that the system be redesigned.

When the problem is structural racism, more fundamental changes are needed, which often is much harder. In the school funding example, one response would be to abandon local revenue sources and fund all public schools in the country at exactly the same level, which would require federal government oversight and revenues, which means additional taxes. Not only would that be opposed by white supremacists, it also goes against the idea that a school functions best with active involvement of not only parents but local communities, which might be undermined by federal intervention.

If uniform public-school funding could be achieved, there are still other hurdles. School districts with wealthier parents, which are disproportionately white, could raise private money to supplement government funding. Would that be allowed? Wealthier parents could enroll their children in private schools. To eliminate that disparity, should we cap private-school spending to the same per-student level as public schools? Should we outlaw private schools altogether?

An even more ambitious approach would be to reduce the racialized wealth gap by redistributionist policies. Since capitalism is a wealth-concentrating system, should we try to tame it with aggressive public policy or must we come up with a new way of organizing economic activity? Until then, should we institute policies that reduce housing segregation by increasing subsidized housing in every wealthy neighborhood?

Whatever one thinks of these potential solutions, they require significant overhauls, not just of public schools but of practices throughout society. The political impediments to such change are formidable, to say the least, as are the technical challenges in implementation if such change were possible.

CASE STUDY: POLICING AND PRISONS

A common focus of the discussion of racism over the past few years has been policing and prisons—the disproportionate use of force,[118] including deadly force,[119] against black and brown people, and the disproportionate rate of incarceration of black and brown people.[120] Are these examples of systemic or structural racism, or both?

First, a critique of the racialized dimension of criminal justice should not detract from a larger concern about how the United States became a "mass incarceration nation" in the last half of the twentieth century.[121] More punitive laws expanding the crimes that lead to prison and jail time, combined with increasing the lengths of sentences, resulted in one of the highest per capita incarceration rates in the world.[122] Independent of racial disparities, many people (including me) believe this is bad public policy.

But part of the story is about race. Many police forces include officers with racist attitudes,[123] but the bigger problem is everyday routines. The problem is not just a few bad cops but a system that leads to police officers targeting black and brown people.[124] When people with white-supremacist assumptions set policy, dictate procedures, and determine best practices, the result is systemic racism. In such a system, even officers of color can participate in practices that produce racist results, such as the case of five black Memphis police officers from a special street-crime unit who in 2022 beat to death Tyre Nichols, a black man stopped for an alleged traffic violation. Such actions fit a pattern of overly aggressive policing in low-income neighborhoods.[125]

What if we were to go deeper and ask about the purpose of the criminal justice system in this society? Once we move beyond rhetoric about keeping people safe—which certainly is one thing policing can accomplish—it's clear that the legal system is also a system of social control in a capitalist economy marked by dramatic wealth inequality.[126]

For example, drug use occurs in every society at every level, but criminalizing drugs has led to law enforcement focusing on poorer people while largely ignoring the affluent, who take fewer risks when buying drugs and have greater resources to fight charges. It's hard to see how existing drug laws have kept people safe. Some critics have suggested that these laws were designed to control the "dangerous classes"[127] that could potentially threaten concentrated wealth. The enforcement of these laws increases racialized wealth inequality[128] and also creates an incarceration economy, in which both owners of private prison corporations[129] and working people who take jobs as guards in public prisons[130] have a stake in protecting this approach to law enforcement.

The current crises in law enforcement and criminal justice are examples of both systemic and structural racism.[131] Changes in hiring and training practices could potentially address the systemic racism. The structural racism poses a more difficult challenge. How much progress can be made in a capitalist system with its inevitable wealth inequality? Capitalism celebrates that inequality as the necessary motivation for innovation and production, allegedly on the way to better lives for everyone. Does the end of white supremacy require the end of capitalism? Without such structural change, are "race-class subjugated communities" always going to be "governed through coercion, containment, repression, surveillance, regulation, predation, discipline, and violence"?[132] Percy Bysshe Shelley is credited with observing, "The rich get richer and the poor get prison," an aphorism so perceptive that it is the title of one of the classic textbooks in criminal justice and criminology, first published in 1979.[133] As one historian puts it, "The best people, with the best of intentions, doing their utmost, cannot fix this system from within."[134]

And if we go deeper, another set of questions emerges: Are any of these changes likely without a simultaneous challenge to the domination/subordination dynamic in patriarchy, which is the foundation of virtually every society? Male dominance—not just centuries but millennia old—was the first social system that justified one group's power over another by claiming such domination is natural. Does the end of white supremacy require the end of patriarchy as well?

WHITE SUPREMACY, NOT WHITENESS

I have repeatedly referred to *white supremacy* but avoided the term *whiteness*. That term is in vogue these days but too often gets used in analytically sloppy fashion. Here's an example.

In an email exchange I was part of, a white educator committed to antiracism criticized an essay about the complex ways our brains make sense of the world.[135] My colleague said such analyses "that ignore or are unaware of how other cultures have looked at this, and only focus on Western science, are practicing whiteness blatantly."

There certainly are varied cultural traditions that provide insights into these questions, but I challenged the conflation of science and whiteness. Modern science emerged out of Europe, but what does it mean to say that practicing modern science is "practicing whiteness"? Other traditions, with systems of knowledge that predate modern science, have much to offer, as I pointed out in Chapter 2, but modern science has expanded human knowledge in ways that are unprecedented. Is that statement, which strikes me as an uncontroversial observation about human history, also an expression of whiteness? If there are people of color who agree with that statement, are they also practicing whiteness?

The essay in question discussed the complexity of the interplay of reason and emotion. In Chapter 2, I quoted feminist philosophers who have challenged a sharp reason/emotion dichotomy. But I wouldn't say it's patriarchal for neuroscientists to pursue these questions using the methods of their discipline. Sexism has shaped modern science in certain ways, as it has shaped every institution in patriarchal societies, but I wouldn't say that the writer of that essay was "practicing maleness" because he focused on neuroscience and ignored feminist philosophy in a short newspaper opinion piece.

This expansive use of "whiteness" as a pejorative can take strange turns. In a news story about the controversy over a professor's argument against affirmative action, one of the sources quoted seemed to challenge the value of academic debate: "This idea of intellectual debate and rigor as the pinnacle of intellectualism comes from a world in which white men dominated."[136] Although the professor quoted has argued that her point has been distorted,[137] what kind of intellectual life is possible if we reject the idea that people with conflicting theories and ideas should seek to resolve the conflict, which implies some kind of debate at some point in an exchange of views? Should we not strive for rigor, the careful assessment of evidence? Collaboration often is the most productive approach to intellectual inquiry, and we don't demand scholarly rigor in every aspect of everyday life. But in intellectual life, as we try to deepen our understanding of how the world works, debate is inevitable and rigor is essential. To label those goals as white and male is counterproductive, not to mention insulting to people of color and women.

Because these kinds of assertions about whiteness are so easy to caricature, reactionary politicians use them to undermine the struggle to press white America to come to terms with systemic and structural racism. Nothing is gained by reducing a complex world to reflexive assertions of good (all things non-white) and bad (anything related to white). That's actually a kind of binary thinking that progressive activists usually tell us to avoid.

Ascribing specific traits to whiteness has become common in one approach to diversity training. The 1999 version of a widely used "White Supremacy Culture" worksheet by Tema Okun[138] offered a list of white characteristics "used as norms and standards without being proactively named or chosen by the group":

perfectionism; sense of urgency; defensiveness; quantity over quality; worship of the written word; only one right way; paternalism; either/or thinking; power hoarding; fear of open conflict; individualism; I'm the only one; progress is bigger, more; objectivity; right to comfort.

Let's consider the question of "objectivity." There are lots of reasons to critique how objectivity norms function in different professions. I've written about the limits of objectivity routines in journalism, suggesting that these routines can actually distort accounts of reality when they lead to giving powerful people a greater voice in defining politics and economics.[139] But objectivity also can mean the attempt to get the most complete account of reality possible by searching for all relevant evidence, which doesn't seem like a bad thing to me. Why is objectivity an outgrowth of whiteness? Would that mean that accepting incomplete accounts of reality is a feature of non-white cultures? Has a person of color who values objectivity been coopted by whiteness?[140]

Okun has said she did not intend people to use her work as a simplistic checklist: "The way it's misused is that people turn it into a checklist to assess or target someone and say: Look, you're exhibiting these characteristics. And that means you're colluding with white supremacy culture, and you're a bad person, you're a terrible person."[141] Understood, but that doesn't negate objections to the overreach of the approach. The 2021 version of the worksheet[142] offered a slightly different list of the markers of White Supremacy Culture and addressed the complexity better. But no matter which version, is it really helpful to make such sweeping generalizations?

Some people argue that narratives are just as important as more formal forms of inquiry designed to produce objectivity, and I agree. We learn a lot from people's stories. But honoring the value of narratives doesn't mean taking everyone's stories at face value without challenge. We are always making judgments about the information we take in, and the concept of objectivity, properly understood, is a good guide for those judgments. Objectivity in that sense doesn't introduce bias but is a corrective to the potential bias that so easily sneaks into our thinking.

These may seem like minor objections, but what is now typically called DEI or DEIB training (diversity, equity, and inclusion; some folks add "belonging") should be rigorous to make such training as effective as possible.[143] That's especially crucial in a time of white backlash, when reactionary forces are eager to caricature attempts to challenge white supremacy. And a lot of diversity training is easy to caricature. When I give talks on racial justice, almost always to multiracial audiences, I often ask, in a faux-earnest voice, "Has anyone ever been in a diversity training that just didn't seem that useful?" That is guaranteed to get a laugh, because almost everyone can remember a long day in a conference room enduring exercises for a DEI training that seemed unfocused, even silly. I don't think that's because diversity training is uniquely done badly but because so many institutional trainings and seminars are poorly designed and boring.

But another part of the problem is that these sessions undertake a task much more complicated than most workplace seminars deal with. DEI trainers aren't teaching people how to use the latest software package or follow new corporate guidelines, but are trying to unravel centuries of oppressive practices deeply embedded in society. That's a heavy lift, especially because "we don't have good evidence for what works," as one research psychologist put it. "We're treating a pandemic of discrimination and racial and religious resentment with untested drugs."[144] That's not a reason to give up but rather motivation for critical self-reflection.[145]

AVOIDING FALSE ALTERNATIVES

Antiracist activists routinely emphasize the need to focus not just on changing the beliefs and actions of racist individuals but on the systems and structural features that embed racism in the culture. Fair enough, but the two are inextricably linked. The collective actions to overhaul or replace a system require the political power to make large-scale change. For movements to assert that kind of political power, they must be large enough to make demands that politicians take seriously, which means persuading more individuals to embrace antiracist politics.

What does all this demand of us? Those of us who believe ourselves to be antiracist need the conviction to remain committed to large-scale change while also being self-critical. People who believe that racial justice already has been achieved need to recognize the need for deeper change. And people who hang onto overtly racist ideas and practices have to be challenged. All these efforts are important.

This is relevant to a common move in progressive politics, to reject the goal that some people (mostly white) articulate of being "colorblind." In a society in which everyone is racialized, positively or negatively, striving to be colorblind in public policy ignores reality. But at the same time, many people (not only white) are trying hard to look past color when they meet someone of a different racial or ethnic group. Many of us are training ourselves to be colorblind, in the sense of rejecting racialized assumptions we have been socialized to make. That's a good thing.

So, a naive claim to be colorblind is obfuscation, especially when it comes to public policy. But good-faith attempts to be colorblind in daily interactions make sense to lots of people. Both things are true, and we have to be able to make these kinds of distinctions.

A social movement doesn't need 100 percent public consensus to make effective change, but racial justice movements need more people on board. Changing the hearts and minds of individuals is part of the process of systemic and structural change, and it requires thoughtful conversations that can resonate with ordinary people, not jargon and dogma. When people say, "I'm trying to be colorblind," the most effective first step might not be to lecture them but to ask, "What do you mean by that?"[146]

The cross-racial coalitions that are required for successful progressive politics demand that white people let go of old stereotypes of people of color and stop imposing those assumptions on them. But in rejecting an old ideology that reduced people of color to lesser-than, we have to avoid creating a new ideology that traps people of color in an identity defined only by color, with an unspoken assumption that their primary role is as judges of all things racial.[147] As a white person, I must never forget the person I'm engaging with is not white, and at the same time never reduce that person to their not-whiteness.[148]

I know that this balancing is hard because I have struggled with it my whole life. The most effective way I know to break through to a more authentic political relationship with people of color is through collective efforts on projects based on shared values. That's a reminder that the struggle for racial justice is advanced not only by campaigns specifically about racial justice but by cross-racial work on other issues, such as justice in economic, global, and sex/gender arenas, as well as efforts to achieve ecological sustainability. In my experience, there is no substitute for time spent together in shared struggle.

THE MESSINESS OF HISTORY AND OUR FUTURE

We need to seek clarity about complexity, carefully. The world is infinitely complex, beyond human abilities to fully understand. So, we simplify. We create categories to organize reality, in order to help us cope with that complexity. That's part of being human, but it requires eternal vigilance to make sure we don't start to believe that our simplifications of reality are reality itself. History is messier than any human theory can account for.

Here's my summary of that messiness: If we want to create a more just and sustainable world, we best keep two things in mind about racism—first, the United States is less racist than ever before, and second, the United States will never overcome white supremacy.

In Chapter 1, I made the simple point that the United States surely is a less racist country than it was in 1958, the year I was born. At the time, the United States was an apartheid society, based on the denial of citizenship to many non-white people. Racist cultural assumptions were the norm, and violent assertions of white supremacy were common in certain regions. Time-travel back to 1958? No thanks. How about 1968, when social movements were struggling to end apartheid? Pick a year, and it's difficult to imagine an argument that we haven't made significant progress, no matter how incomplete the project, in combatting white supremacy in my lifetime. It's important to acknowledge this progress if we want to be effective politically, and to honor the many people who struggled, suffered, took risks, and sometimes gave their lives to end American apartheid.

The argument that the United States will never overcome white supremacy is less obvious. I don't mean that a progressive politics is doomed to fail, but rather that if white society could let go of white supremacy in all its manifestations, we would be such a radically different country that we wouldn't recognize ourselves. If that sounds ridiculous, consider US history.

The land base and the phenomenal wealth of the United States are based on the almost complete extermination of the indigenous population to establish the country; African slavery to create the wealth that propelled the nation into the industrial era; and the twentieth-century exploitation of developing countries, often imposed through military force. These three racialized holocausts have made the country the richest in the history of the world. All those holocaust-level crimes—involving millions of deaths, incalculable suffering, and the destruction of entire societies—were motivated by desires for wealth and power but justified by, and made politically possible because of, white supremacy. We will not transcend white supremacy until we can collectively tell the truth about those crimes. The society that could ever get to that place would be, I suspect, so different from the country we live in that it wouldn't be the same country.

We've taken significant steps toward racial justice, and a long struggle lies ahead. Both things are true and both things are relevant in trying to understand a complex world.

Social movements challenging deeply entrenched injustice need to be honest about the difficulty of that struggle. At the same time, those movements have to help people imagine that the more radical change in unjust systems is possible. Organizers develop strategies and slogans that emphasize *Sí, se puede* ("Yes, we can," the slogan of the United Farm Workers), even when success is unlikely, at least in the short term.

Strategies and slogans designed to motivate people, especially to stay committed over the long haul, are important. But those strategies should be based on careful assessment of the level of change needed to reach a goal and the impediments to that change. That analysis is aided by clarity in definitions, which is necessary to counter the tendency toward jargon and dogma that creates a sense of in-group belonging.

I realize this analysis reflects my personality. I like precision in language. I'm not energized by chants. When someone offers a slogan, my instinct is not to repeat it but to ask what it means. Both aspects of the human animal—the desire to come together with others in a cause that lifts our spirits, and the quest to deepen our understanding of a complex world—are important ingredients in the struggle for a better world.

CRITICAL RACE THEORY

By the way, is this analysis an example of critical race theory? I waited until the end of this chapter to raise the question because attaching that label up front might lead to automatic rejection by many people in conservative politics and the Republican Party. Rather than try to determine whether my arguments fit in a category that has been caricatured and demonized by right-wing activists,[149] it would be better to assess my arguments on their merit.

Some parts of this chapter clearly fit under the CRT umbrella. I agree that social, political, and economic institutions are not neutral in regard to race, and analyses of systemic and structural racism are at the heart of CRT. Other aspects of this chapter may not be embraced by all those who count themselves as in the CRT camp, which doesn't have a specific set of doctrines one must embrace to be part of the struggle.

The formal launching of a CRT movement is usually identified as a 1989 conference titled "New Developments in Critical Race Theory," mainly focused on the law. Challenges to the notion of legal neutrality go back at least to the legal realism movement of the early twentieth century, which understood law as an outgrowth of economic and political forces rather than neutral principles that float above social systems. The critical legal studies movement that started in the 1970s offered a more radical critique of the effect of oppressive systems of power on law. Feminist critiques of the patriarchal character of the law emerged in about the same time period. CRT is part of a rich tradition of critical thinking, something most educators endorse.

I remember encountering all of these ideas during my time in graduate school (1988–92), during which I began to see that I had unconsciously accepted the society's conventional wisdom about power and the distribution of wealth. Before that, I would have said that there are serious problems in equality and equity but that they could be solved by the traditions and institutions put in place by our Founding Fathers, if we apply the rules fairly.

My shift to a more critical perspective was not a purely intellectual exercise, of course. As I argued in Chapter 2, we shouldn't think of what we call reason and emotion as completely separate endeavors. As I learned more about US history and the way institutions work, I had to deal with discomfort. I take that experience to be an indication of growth, both intellectual and personal. As a result, when Florida passed the Stop WOKE (Wrongs to Our Kids and Employees) Act in 2022, I was particularly struck by one section of this law that sort of makes it illegal to require any student to participate in educational activities involving critical approaches to US history and society. (I say "sort of" because the law is vague, overbroad, and largely incoherent, suggesting it was designed to further political goals rather than to improve education.) What caught my eye was the law's claim to protect people from feeling "guilt, anguish, or other forms of psychological distress because of actions, in which the individual played no part, committed in the past by other members of the same race, color, sex, or national origin."[150]

At various times, up to the present, I have felt distress when learning about the myriad ways I have benefited from being white, of European heritage, male, and a US citizen. The distress is a result of recognizing the unfairness of the systems I live in. I have not felt guilty about—in the sense of being personally responsible for—historical events such as slavery (I was not alive when slavery was legal) or racialized police violence (I've never worked in law enforcement or supported mass-incarceration policies). But I have felt guilty over racist jokes I told in the past, or times when I know I should have stood up for justice but stepped back out of fear. Feeling guilty—in the sense of an awareness of not meeting my own moral standards—about my failures is appropriate. And I feel anguish every day because of the suffering that results from racism, sexism, and other forms of injustice, no matter what my connection to that suffering.

I manage to handle all that, and so can students. Educators in New York created a pilot unit for an Advanced Placement high school government class that had students debate the history of racism and CRT. In feedback from students, half of them white and half students of color, none disparaged the country or sought to evoke white guilt. Many were passionate about resisting attempts to limit what they could study, with comments such as "It's not right to pass laws saying we can't learn about it in school" and "What is education if we erase history?" The researchers observed that students were "intellectually stimulated by engaging in open discussion and drawing their own evidenced-based conclusions."[151]

Psychological discomfort about human suffering is an indication that one takes seriously foundational moral principles, such as the inherent dignity of all people and the need for social solidarity. Just as physical pain is an indication of something wrong in the body, psychological discomfort can be an indication that there is something wrong in the body politic. To outlaw such discomfort is to make both accurate history and moral progress impossible. Reactionary right-wing organizations and much of the Republican Party in the United States have embraced an identity that is anti-intellectual by trying to shut down critical thinking, and amoral by trying to detach politics from moral imperatives.

If that seems harsh to conservative readers, their challenge is to explain what in this chapter is factually inaccurate or logically unsound. In the next chapter I will offer the same challenge to liberal/progressive/left people on questions of sex and gender.

Chapter 5:
Defining Sex/Gender: Beyond Trans Ideology

A NOTE TO READERS

This is where, in the original manuscript of this book, readers would have found Chapter 5, "Defining Sex/Gender: Beyond Trans Ideology." Here's the story of why it's not here.

The editors at Interlink Publishing/Olive Branch Press raised objections to the analysis and political implications of that chapter. They told me that they wanted to publish the book but, in good conscience, couldn't do so with this chapter because of their support for the goals of the transgender movement. I understood their concerns and also wanted them to publish the book, given their excellent work and the positive relationship we had built. Still, I believed that chapter was integral to the book. We potentially were at an impasse. But after a constructive conversation, I agreed to drop that chapter from the published book. In turn, Interlink agreed to allow me to explain the process and direct readers to my website (https://robertwjensen.org/), where they can read the missing chapter for free.

Interlink Publishing has a long history of supporting LGBTQIA+ rights. You can read the note from the publisher about Interlink's decision to publish the book, despite their profound disagreement with me on this issue, by visiting this page on their website (https://www.interlinkbooks.com/itsdebatable_note/).

I am grateful that Interlink didn't pursue a scorched-earth policy and reject all of my writing on the basis of a disagreement on one issue, something I have experienced with some critics in the past. (For details, see the Conclusion.)

Several times in this book I have asserted that "reasonable people can disagree" and continue a healthy and productive conversation. I believe the way that Interlink and I resolved this disagreement is an example of that.

Chapter 6:
Defining Ecological Sustainability:
Fewer and Less

In one of his Sabbath poems, Wendell Berry offers this advice for responding to the young when they ask the old about hope: "What will you tell them? Tell them at least what you say to yourself."[152]

I remember the first time I told a class at the University of Texas what I say to myself about the future, probably sometime around 2005. (My memory for dates is fading fast.)

I don't remember what the topic of discussion was that day, nor can I recall what prompted my remarks. But in an honors seminar that focused on the responsibility of intellectuals (a framework that many have borrowed from Noam Chomsky[153]), we wandered into a discussion of the ecological crises. (I loved teaching that class, in large part because I designed it to provide plenty of room to wander.) Without planning it, I said something like this:

> I grew up in a world of endless bounty and expanding material prosperity, with a belief in perpetual economic growth. My generation was told there would always be more, and the task was figuring out how to share it with everyone in the world. The moral challenge for us was how to solve the inequality problem and figure out how to feed the world. Your generation is growing up in a world that is going to be defined not by expansion but by contraction, and

it's not going to be easy to share more equitably when there is less of everything. I think the moral challenge for you, assuming that you continue to live in an affluent country like the United States, is how to cope with living in the midst of a massive, slow-moving human die-off in other parts of the world. You will have to figure out how to live through a period of human suffering that we cannot imagine.

The room was quiet. I doubt all the thirty students in the class agreed with my assessment, but no one scoffed or tried to make a joke. I didn't see a reason to press the matter, and no one looked eager to continue. After a moment of quiet reflection, we moved on. But one student came to my office later that day to thank me. "I think about that kind of thing all the time," she said. "It is nice to know I'm not crazy."

Those thoughts were not crazy then, and they are certainly not crazy today. But a few caveats are necessary.

First, I wasn't predicting when or how such a state of affairs might come to be. I was simply noting that the trajectory of the human species is moving toward such an outcome, not in some science-fiction future but quite possibly in this century, within the lifetime of my students.

Second, I wasn't suggesting that people haven't faced overwhelming moral challenges in the past. Human suffering that most people cannot imagine is part of various epochs in human history, and it is part of life today. But the global nature of catastrophic ecological collapse will be unprecedented.

Third, I wasn't arguing that the extreme inequality in the distribution of wealth today was trivial or unworthy of our attention. But focusing on that inequality today, which we have an obligation to do, won't automatically lead to an ecologically sustainable human presence on Earth.

That experience led me to be a bit bolder in raising these points in front of progressive groups I was part of. Instead of thinking about discrete environmental problems and discrete solutions, I began to think more about warnings from ecologists, captured in the ideas of our ecological footprint[154] and the overarching problem of overshoot[155]—when a population exceeds the capacity of its territory to generate the resources necessary for life, to process its wastes, and to provide adequate space for activities. Instead of looking only at the failures of specific political and economic systems, I started pondering the "temptations of dense energy" that are at the heart of out-of-control growth.

In 2008, I gave a talk titled "The Old Future's Gone: Progressive Strategy amid Cascading Crises" to an interfaith social justice group.[156] In 2011, I spoke on "Nature Bats Last: Notes on Revolution and Resistance, Revelation and Redemption" at a peace group's convention.[157] In a 2013 lecture at a Unitarian church, I started using the phrase "We are all apocalyptic now."[158]

Around this same time, I got to know Wes Jackson, cofounder of The Land Institute, who has been an important thinker in the sustainable agriculture and environmental education movements since the 1970s. Our work together pushed me to face the multiple cascading crises without false hope, and Jackson and I published a book in 2022 that describes one approach to that kind of reckoning.[159]

In this chapter, I want to lay out a framework that draws on all this work and explains why I was so blunt with my students all those years ago. I am aware that I am out of step not only with the political projects of the Republican and Democratic parties but also with much of the environmental movement and the political left, which makes it more important to present this analysis.

In previous chapters, I have outlined political positions that are controversial mostly on one side of the political fence. My writing about the enduring white supremacy in the United States draws criticism mainly from the right—though not everyone on the left would agree with every aspect of my analysis, and some conservatives might agree with parts of it. My writing about ideology of transgenderism draws criticism mainly from the left—though conservatives don't necessarily agree with the radical feminist framework I endorse, and some leftists agree with me. But critics of my writing on ecology have come from every part of the political spectrum: right, center, and left. Why the equal-opportunity rejection?

My guess is, because I do not believe there are solutions to the multiple cascading crises of our moment in history—if by solutions we mean ways to sustain eight billion people on Earth, let alone eight billion people with a significant number of them continuing to live in high-energy/high-technology societies. Jackson and I suggested in *An Inconvenient Apocalypse* that we need to prepare for a future of "fewer and less"—fewer people consuming less stuff.[160] That's a vision that isn't widely popular.

THREE REVOLUTIONS

To think about a new future, we need to understand the present. To do that, let's highlight the three major revolutions—agricultural, industrial, and delusional—that brought us to this moment in human history.[161]

These are not revolutions in the sense of political/military campaigns that have relatively clear starting and ending points. Nor are they revolutions that happened only in one place or under any organized direction. But they are revolutions in the sense of dramatic changes, decisive breaks with the past that changed the trajectory of human history.

The *agricultural revolution* started about ten thousand years ago when a gathering-hunting species discovered how to cultivate plants for food. Two crucial things resulted from that, one ecological and one political.

Ecologically, the invention of agriculture kicked off an intensive human assault on natural systems. By that I don't mean that gathering-hunting humans never did damage to local ecosystems, but only that the large-scale destruction we cope with today has its origins in agriculture. Humans exhausting the energy-rich carbon of the soil turned out to be the first step in the road to extractive economies that deplete resources beyond replacement levels. After agriculture, humans felled forests to provide the energy to smelt copper, bronze, and iron. Then came coal, oil, and natural gas. I also don't mean that all agriculture is equally destructive. Given the varied geography and geology of Earth, human agricultural practices vary from place to place. But large-scale annual grain agriculture (crops such as wheat, rice, and corn—the staples of human diets for thousands of years) has required plowing that leads to soil erosion and depletion, and has never been sustainable over the long term.

Politically, agriculture produced the first large-scale surpluses in human history.[162] The ability to stockpile food made possible concentrations of power that generally were foreign to gathering-hunting societies, which led to social hierarchies, starting with patriarchy. Again, this is not to say that humans were not capable of doing bad things to each other prior to agriculture, but only that what we understand as institutionalized oppression has its roots in agriculture. We need not romanticize pre-agricultural life to recognize the ways in which agriculture made possible dramatically different levels of unsustainability and injustice.

A brief digression: It's fashionable on the left to challenge this account, as seen in the enthusiastic reaction to the 2021 book *The Dawn of Everything: A New History of Humanity*.[163] David Graeber and David Wengrow point out that there have been societies that don't fit this generalization about human history in all respects, which is not surprising given that there are no "laws" of human behavior as there are laws of physics and chemistry. But there are patterns in history, which vary based on differences in geography, climate, and environmental conditions. Exceptions to patterns can help us see the range of options for the future, but they don't negate the forces that create the patterns. We learn most from patterns, not exceptions. The exceptions tell us what is possible, but the patterns tell us what forces are most powerful. That book's challenge to the centrality of agriculture in changing the course of human history is unpersuasive because it ignores those patterns.

The *industrial revolution* that took off in eighteenth-century Europe intensified the human assault on ecosystems and on each other. Water and wind power played an early role in this revolution, but the unleashing of the concentrated energy of coal, oil, and natural gas kicked things into high gear. This machine-based world has produced unparalleled material comfort for some. Whatever one thinks of the effect of such comforts on human psychology and societies (and in my view, the effect has been mixed), the processes that produce the comfort are destroying the capacity of the ecosphere to sustain large-scale human life as we know it into the future, and in the present those comforts are not distributed in a fashion consistent with any meaningful conception of justice. In short, the way we live is in direct conflict with common sense and the ethical principles on which we claim to base our lives. How is that possible?

The *delusional revolution* is my term for the everyday practices and habits of thought generated by unprecedented levels of material comfort. This dense-energy-driven acquisitiveness has been intensified by the development in the twentieth century of sophisticated propaganda techniques—what we politely refer to as marketing and advertising. These levels of comfort have come to be seen as normal in developed societies, while many people in less affluent societies aspire to that comfort. When people begin to believe those comforts are necessities, we find it easy to overlook the costs. Marketing and advertising do their best to make sure we never think about the costs, that we accept the delusion that endless expansion on a finite planet is possible.

The pathological profit motive in capitalism is part of the delusional story, but hardly the whole story. At the heart of this is what Jackson and I call the "temptations of dense energy," the way in which the industrial revolution created new expectations for material goods and levels of comfort in everyday life. Even those of us who try to resist it often can't help but be drawn into parts of the delusion. As a culture, we collectively end up acting as if unsustainable systems can be sustained because we want them to be. Much of the culture's storytelling—whether through the corporations that dominate mass media or the individuals who generate social media—remains committed to maintaining this delusional state. In such a culture, it becomes hard to extract oneself from that story.

In summary: The agricultural revolution set us on a road to destruction. The industrial revolution ramped up our speed. The delusional revolution has prevented us from coming to terms with the reality of who we've become and where we are heading. That's the bad news. The worse news is that there's still overwhelming resistance to acknowledging that these kinds of discussions are necessary, both in mainstream institutions and in the social movements that critique the dominant culture.

THE OLD FUTURE IS GONE

The phrase I used in the title of that 2008 talk, "The old future is gone," is borrowed from singer-songwriter John Gorka: "The old future's dead and gone/Never to return/There's a new way through the hills ahead/This one we'll have to earn."[164]

The old future of endless expansion is over, but no one can offer more than a tentative sketch of the transition to a new future of contraction. We can't know the exact way through the hills or predict all of the challenges we will face as we try to earn that future. I believe that's a key reason most people—including those who are passionately committed to ecological sustainability and social justice—reject "fewer and less" as the goal. It's too uncertain and too uncomfortable to ponder.

Of course, reasonable people can disagree, and I could be wrong. Some people, including very smart people I respect, believe that we can find a way out of the problems in which the modern world is ensnared. For example, a leading liberal economist suggests that a few years ago we had reason to believe a reduction in consumption was necessary:

> But huge progress in renewable energy and related technologies, notably batteries, means that it now looks almost easy to achieve a low-emission economy. We can now easily envision a society in which people drive electric vehicles and cook on induction ranges, using power generated by solar panels and wind turbines, and experience no sense of sacrifice.[165]

"Almost easy"? "No sense of sacrifice"? I don't find such glib reassurances reassuring, especially when we recognize that most of the ecological crises are the result of "progress traps"[166]—the problems we inadvertently introduce when seeking to improve our lives, which we then can't solve. Ronald Wright coined the term to describe:

> a chain of successes which, upon reaching a certain scale, leads to disaster. The dangers are seldom seen before it's too late. The jaws of a trap open slowly and invitingly, then snap closed fast.[167]

Human successes in what Wes Jackson calls the "scramble for energy-rich carbon," from agriculture through the fossil-fuel era, have led to profound human failures in our treatment of each other and our care for the larger living world. The jaws opened slowly but now threaten to snap closed much faster than we can deal with.

Some people may focus on specific traps, such as rapid climate destabilization, but any specific ecological crisis should be understood as a derivative of overshoot—too many people consuming too much in the aggregate.

Here's a simple timeline from my life to help us grasp the scale. My father was born in 1927, when the world population was two billion. In 1974, the midpoint of his life, we hit four billion. When he died at the end of 2022, the world population was eight billion. In one person's lifetime, just three generations, the world population doubled and doubled again. That's unprecedented, as was the increase in energy consumption. In the twentieth century, the average annual per capita supply of commercial energy more than quadrupled.[168] That consumption also is marked by inequality; at the end of that century, 10 percent of the world's population consumed more than 40 percent of commercial primary energy, and the bottom 50 percent of the population had access to about 10 percent of the energy.[169]

Also unprecedented are the effects on the ecosphere of all those people consuming all that energy. Virtually every ecosystem on Earth has been degraded by this level of human habitation. A 2019 UN report shows that three-quarters of the land-based environment and two-thirds of the marine environment have been significantly altered by human actions.[170] Such studies now appear regularly in the news. "A 'Crossroads' for Humanity: Earth's Biodiversity Is Still Collapsing"[171] described a 2020 report from the UN Convention on Biodiversity that reminds us species extinction is not only unfortunate for the species that go extinct but also threatens humanity's food supply, health, and security.[172] A study published the following year concluded that only 3 percent of the land surface is "faunally intact."[173]

Politics and economics have yet to adapt to this. In 2022, a respected think tank warns that "To Prevent the Collapse of Biodiversity, the

World Needs a New Planetary Politics."[174] Even if one's focus is on the economic bottom line, such as the folks at the World Economic Forum in 2023, it's hard not to notice: "Terrestrial and marine ecosystems are facing multiple pressure points due to their undervalued contribution to the global economy as well as overall planetary health."[175]

The rate of population growth is slowing, due in large part to advances in the status of women and education of girls, but growth is predicted through this century, peaking at perhaps ten billion.[176] Slowing growth is of little comfort. Even if we were to reduce per capita consumption worldwide, especially in affluent countries, all three potential population scenarios pose problems.

- A growing global population poses serious challenges for humanity by intensifying the consequences of overshoot. That means greater social instability and more rapid ecological degradation.
- A stable global population poses serious challenges for humanity, since we are already in overshoot. That means, at the very least, existing levels of social instability and ecological degradation can be expected to continue.
- A shrinking global population poses serious challenges for humanity, given that the world economy is built on overshoot.

By the 2020s, politicians routinely were raising alarms about how falling birth rates in affluent societies raise the elderly dependency ratio (the ratio of working people to older folks; a high dependency ratio means that fewer young people carry a heavier burden to support those who are not economically active). Slowing population growth risks the economic growth on which virtually all of the world economy is based. Even China, once the country working hardest to restrict births, is concerned.

Many of my friends and allies in progressive movements reject any concerns about population, dismissing them as neo-Malthusian,[177] as if Thomas Malthus's inaccurate predictions about food production in the nineteenth century mean we need not worry about the question today.[178] Many on the left avoid the question because of the racist and ethnocentric ideologies that have been associated with concerns about overpopulation in the past, and unfortunately continue today in what is being called the "ecofascist" movement,[179] defined as "a kind of environmentalism that advocates violence or the exclusion of some groups of people due to their race or class—or both."[180] That doesn't mean there is no overpopulation problem, only that we must be careful to avoid bad analysis and ugly politics.[181]

The problem of too many humans should not be blamed on poor or non-white people in the developing world. It's a problem created by the trajectory of human history, the result of our ability to get at more and more energy-rich carbon with new technologies, leading to ecological degradation resulting from too many people consuming too much overall. That brings us to the second part of "fewer and less," the need to reduce aggregate consumption.

DENSE ENERGY'S TEMPTATIONS

This discussion should start with the problem of an inequitable distribution of wealth in the world today, both within societies and between societies. In the United States, relatively few people and corporations control too much of the country's wealth. The United States and other developed countries control too much of the world's wealth.

But even if we could achieve an equitable distribution of wealth, within the United States and worldwide, the current level of aggregate consumption would be unsustainable. People on the bottom, those consuming the least amount of energy, need more to reach a minimally decent standard of living. But everyone else needs to consume much less. What does that mean for a society such as the United States?

Let's start with the billionaires: In a sustainable world, there would be no billionaires. There also would be no millionaires, no upper middle class, no middle class. The consumption of virtually everyone in the United States, except for those living the most precariously, would have to drop.

How hard can that be? Incredibly hard, not just because of corporate greed or crafty advertisers but because of those temptations of dense energy. We could start by eliminating the most obviously wasteful uses of resources—let's say a ban on private jets and cruise vacations. That's easy to imagine, at least for those of us who don't fly on private jets and don't want to take a cruise. But how about grounding almost all air travel and severely curtailing long-distance car travel? That is harder to imagine, not because we couldn't live without airplanes and cars but because we've built a world in which those things are a part of "normal" life.

The people who fly and drive are not uniquely bad people (at least, I hope they aren't, because I used to fly a lot for work and politics, and I still drive a car). What once were luxuries have become more widely available, eventually becoming part of everyday life for almost everyone who can afford them. If we are to reduce our consumption to a sustainable level, we have a hard discussion ahead of how easily the things we *want* become the things we believe we *need*, of how difficult it is to give up that dense energy. Planes, cars, electronics, large single-family houses, easy access to foods from around the world—none of these things are going to be normal in the human future, if there is to be a human future.

Some uses of energy and material resources are frivolous and wasteful by any standards—it's hard to imagine anyone making a serious argument that yachts are essential to human thriving—but many uses of energy simply make our lives easier. Here's my favorite example.

Imagine that you need to dig a trench to put in a water line from a well to your home. That water pipe has to be below the frost line, which in northern New Mexico where I live used to be about five feet down. From the well to my house is more than three hundred feet, let's call it the length of a football field. Part of the reason for the distance is the setback rule from the septic system, necessary if we want an indoor toilet, which is quite a bit handier than an outhouse, especially in the winter. That trench, by the way, also carries the wires that power the electric well pump, necessary if I don't want to pump water by hand. Back to the trench: You can dig that by hand with a shovel or use a backhoe. Digging by hand would take weeks for one person. Fire up the backhoe, and you're done in a day, with no backache. Which do you choose?

Even the modest home I live in—like all the modern infrastructure most of us tend to take for granted, up to the level we can afford—is dependent on the highly dense carbon found in fossil fuels. The current fantasy that electrifying everything will solve our problems, reflected in the comments of the economist quoted earlier, ignores the realities that not everything can be electrified in a sustainable manner and that the extraction of resources to construct renewable-energy infrastructure requires fossil fuel.[182]

And then there's our food.[183] Folks who deny that Earth is overpopulated with humans like to point out that there's a lot of food in the world, enough to feed all eight billion people if equitably distributed. That's true, for now, but why is agriculture so productive? Largely because of "fuel and electricity inputs used directly by field machines and by irrigation, and indirectly to produce machinery and agricultural chemicals, above all to synthesize nitrogen fertilizers." Vaclav Smil, one of the world's experts on energy, calculates the results of using all that energy:

> Global harvest now supports, on the average, 4 people per hectare of cropland, compared to about 1.5 person in 1900. Best performances are much higher: 20 people/hectare in The Netherlands, 17 in China's most populous provinces, 12 in the United States on a rich diet and with large-scale food exports.[184]

Much of the extraordinary population increase is the result of that industrial production of anhydrous ammonia as a source of nitrogen fertilizer for modern agriculture. In the late nineteenth century, it was clear that supplies of natural fertilizers such as guano were being rapidly exhausted. The Haber-Bosch process, invented in the early twentieth century, was revolutionary, "solving" the problem of where to find enough nitrogen for soils depleted by intensive agriculture.[185] Scholars estimate that this industrial process, which typically uses natural gas as the feedstock to turn tightly bonded atmospheric nitrogen into ammonia, supports nearly half the world's population.[186] But because those nitrogen bonds in the air are so tight, the process takes a lot of energy. A disruption in the supply of energy would mean a worldwide famine of unprecedented proportions. But continuing to burn all that fossil fuel accelerates global warming.

What's the solution? In the old future that assumed endless expansion, we believed that there were always solutions waiting to be invented. In the new future of limits, serious talk of solutions should start with fewer and less. At risk of being annoying, remember that rapid climate disruption, while a huge problem, is not the only problem.[187] Climate change is a derivative of the foundational ecological problem of overshoot—we have exceeded the long-term carrying capacity of Earth and are degrading the biophysical basis of our own existence.

But wait, say those holding onto the old future, our species is quite inventive. Human creativity and ingenuity can solve, and have solved, many problems, often in ways that couldn't have been predicted even a few years before those inventions. After all, Malthus and others have long predicted massive human starvation, but we've found ways to expand food production. The Haber-Bosch process is an example of that "success."

Well, sort of. Yes, modern agricultural science, along with the Haber-Bosch process, have doubled and tripled yields per acre of our major grain crops. But the widespread use of these fertilizers in an increasingly industrialized agriculture means that after being spread over millions of acres of grain-producing fields, the surplus industrial nitrogen finds its way into waterways until it meets the ocean waters, where it creates huge dead zones. On the way downriver, cities spend millions of dollars to remove it from drinking water, in some places failing so dramatically that people have to drink bottled water.[188]

And nitrogen isn't the only problem. There also are problems, both of shortages and excess, with phosphorus, another essential element for plant growth. The world is running out of phosphorus, with experts estimating "peak phosphorus" coming within decades. Meanwhile, the excess from agricultural runoff leads to toxic algae blooms. Researchers estimate that Florida's Lake Okeechobee receives about ten times what that lake can safely take in, and harmful algal blooms also plague the sources for some cities' drinking water, such as Lake Erie.[189]

Meanwhile, annual plowing of the vast acres used to grow crucial grains such as wheat means continuing soil erosion. Worldwide, about 23 billion tons a year erode beyond replacement levels, which is about 0.7 percent of the world's soil inventory.[190] Take a minute to do the math, and it's sobering to realize that at the current rate of erosion there would be no topsoil in about 150 years. How do we figure those costs into our evaluation of the "success" of industrial agriculture?

If we were to follow ecologist Stan Rowe's advice and define progress as "whatever is conducive to sustainable participation in Earth's ecosystems,"[191] we would have to rethink our constant clamoring for progress-as-more. High-energy/high-technology can solve problems, but it almost always creates other problems—that's the law of unintended consequences.[192] Yet as a society, we too often ignore that particular pattern in history. As a society, we are in the grip of what in the previous chapter I labeled technological fundamentalism, the belief that we can solve all problems through new gadgets, including the problems created by old gadgets. If techno-optimists don't like being called fundamentalists, we could call this techno-worship "solutionism," which Evgeny Morozov borrows from urban planning and architecture to describe "an unhealthy preoccupation with sexy, monumental, and narrow-minded solutions— the kind of stuff that wows audiences at TED conferences—to problems that are extremely complex, fluid, and contentious."[193]

Whatever term we use, both right and left have faith in the promise of technological fixes, which sometimes feels a lot like a religion.

WE ARE NOT GODS

Is it fair to suggest this techno-optimism is a new version of that old-time religion? Here's an example, from an environmentalist who proclaims that natural forces no longer run Earth—humans do. That's a way of saying we are gods, which isn't my interpretation but rather the book's title, *The God Species: Saving the Planet in the Age of Humans*. Claiming that this God-status is a necessity, he argues:

> Central to the standard Green creed is the idea that playing God is
> dangerous. Hence the reflexive opposition to new technologies from
> splitting the atom to cloning cattle. My thesis is the reverse: playing
> God (in the sense of being intelligent designers) at a planetary level
> is essential if creation is not to be irreparably damaged or even

destroyed by humans unwittingly deploying our newfound powers in disastrous ways. At this late stage, false humility is a more urgent danger than hubris. The truth of the Anthropocene is that the Earth is far out of balance, and we must help it regain the stability it needs to function as a self-regulating, highly dynamic, and complex system. It cannot do so alone.[194]

Mark Lynas is an environmentalist, not a corporate profiteer or shill for the wealthy who is trying to rationalize the destruction of a living world for the sake of profit. He co-founded the "pro-science environmental campaign network" RePlanct, described as "a new kind of environmental movement with a radical, science-backed plan to repair the damage to our precious starship Earth."[195] Based on Lynas's arguments, it's seems that "pro-science" and "science-backed" are synonyms for technological fundamentalism.

There is a painful irony in this kind of talk. These fundamentalists are confident we can do almost anything we set our minds to—except devise and implement a plan to reduce population and consumption, the most effective ways to respond to the multiple cascading crises. The techno-optimist solutionism is necessary because we can't seem to come up with ways to move toward fewer and less. We are funny kinds of gods, if we can do everything except control our own behavior.

I understand why it's attractive to believe in technical fixes to the problems that the industrial economy has created through its relentless extraction of material resources. But is that a sensible approach? Technological fundamentalists believe that the increasing use of ever more sophisticated high-energy advanced technology is always a good thing and that any problems caused by previous high-tech "solutions" eventually can be remedied by more technology. Perhaps the ultimate example of this fundamentalism is geo-engineering, the belief that we can intervene in the climate system at the planetary level to deal with global warming. Given massive human failure at much lower levels of intervention, this approach—for example, what is called "solar radiation management," which would inject sulfate aerosols into the stratosphere to reflect back sunlight—seems, quite literally, crazy.

Am I unfair in my assessment? Let's go back to Lynas, who is one of the sort-of environmentalists who produced the "Ecomodernist Manifesto," which argues:

> Intensifying many human activities—particularly farming, energy extraction, forestry, and settlement—so that they use less land and interfere less with the natural world is the key to decoupling human development from environmental impacts. These socioeconomic and technological processes are central to economic modernization and environmental protection. Together they allow people to mitigate climate change, to spare nature, and to alleviate global poverty.[196]

The ecomodernists believe in applying human ingenuity to long-term planning, just not the kind of planning that could lead to reducing aggregate consumption. Instead, they bet we can keep drawing down the ecological capital of the planet beyond replacement levels—indeed, even intensify the drawdown—because we will magically decouple our consumption from the material world through more and better gadgets. In other words, we really are gods—we can create what we want, out of the void.

Again, I am not unfairly slapping a pejorative label on the ecomodernists. Another of the manifesto's co-authors, Stewart Brand of *Whole Earth Catalog* fame, wrote in 1968, "We are as gods and might as well get good at it."[197] Forty years later, he updated that: "We are as gods and HAVE to get good at it."[198] Brand's god-like imagination includes what he calls "de-extinction science" and "resurrection biology," using new tools in synthetic biology "to liberate conservation in a spectacular way" and "to bring some extinct species back to life."[199] Ponder the application of the law of unintended consequences to that project.

Should humans seek to be gods from science fiction or should we embrace ecological realism? After a century of mounting failures of technological fundamentalism, the ecomodernists encourage us to double down on grandiose projects and magical thinking, all in the name of science. Remaking the planet and remaking life—what could possibly go wrong?

Most environmentalists I know would reject this kind of exuberant rhetoric. But most of them also reject any discussion of population size, preferring to focus only on first-world consumption. Here's an example.

A friend recently told me he had no doubt that Earth could support eight billion people if per capita energy consumption of the richest countries dropped to the average level of the poorest. I said that beyond the political problem of achieving such equality and fairness, I believed such arrangements still would be unsustainable. There are no equations that answer such questions definitively, but research and common sense can guide us. I asked him, do you think the world could support eighty billion people? He laughed and said no. So, the number of people Earth can sustain is not infinite? He agreed. Then on what basis, I asked, have you concluded that eight billion is sustainable, other than that it feels reassuring? He had no answer, but countered, appropriately, that my conclusion also wasn't definitive. I agreed that no one knows the answer, but that ecologists whom I trust have long said that two billion is a reasonable target for a sustainable human population.[200]

Whatever the number, in the absence of a compelling argument that the current population and aggregate consumption are sustainable, "fewer and less" is the responsible project. We don't need an exact number, which is beyond anyone's predictive capacity, to know the direction we must move. I have never seen a claim that the current population or higher is sustainable that didn't rest on what one writer calls "rescue remedies" that are attractive only because we are caught up "in our heedless rush toward a chimerical techno nirvana."[201]

Capitalists are more likely to embrace this techno-optimism openly, reflected in former ExxonMobil CEO Rex Tillerson's 2012 comment about climate change: "It's an engineering problem, and it has engineering solutions."[202] But unless socialists are willing to confront the need for limits, whether they like it or not, they are betting that Tillerson is right.

SOCIALISM WON'T SAVE US

Since I have not hidden my opposition to capitalism, some readers might wonder why I have not pinned the blame for ecological crises on that economic system and its profit-driven demand for growth without concern for long-term consequences. As many have pointed out, capitalism runs on the logic of a cancer cell, an obsession with growth that will eventually kill the host.[203]

Capitalism's defenders tend to avoid that challenge and redirect attention to the unprecedented innovation of the capitalist era and the extraordinary expansion of material wealth, albeit unevenly distributed. Depending on their ideological camp, capitalists argue that perhaps some light government regulation can fix market failures and correct the course. Other capitalists argue for removing what little regulation exists to liberate the creativity of markets more fully. Waiting in the right-wings are the technological solutions.

Socialist critics argue that innovation is possible in more collaborative systems and that vast wealth inequality and ecological destruction is inevitable in capitalism. Instead of production for profit and a growth economy, we need production for people in an economy that does not undermine the health of ecosystems. Waiting in the left-wings are the technological solutions.

I see no future in capitalism because the logic of a system premised on infinite growth does not allow for fewer and less. Technology will not save us.

I see no future in socialism unless we change not only our economics but also our expectations and embrace fewer and less. Technology will not save us.

Let me illustrate these points with stories about my communication with two readers of *An Inconvenient Apocalypse*, both smart people whom I respect, one libertarian and the other socialist.

The libertarian and I agreed that no combination of renewable energy sources can replace the concentrated energy of the fossil fuels on which contemporary society is based.[204] Because he is not a climate-change denier, he also acknowledged that there's a strong argument that we must down-power to reduce ecological damage. However, because he couldn't imagine a political program to accomplish that, he argued we have no choice but to bet on capitalism and technological fixes, continuing to exploit fossil fuels and nuclear energy until there is a viable alternative that allows business as usual.

The socialist and I agreed that replacing capitalism with an economic system that rejected wealth concentration and focused on human needs was essential. He also acknowledged that there's a strong argument that we must down-power to reduce ecological damage. He argued that a truly democratic socialism would make that more likely than a superficially democratic capitalism, but he could not explain how socialism would magically make people ignore those temptations of dense energy.

Again, so I'm not misunderstood: I am not neutral on the question of how to structure an economy; I see no plausible human future in capitalism, and I think democratic socialism offers us a way forward—but only if we collectively agree to set dramatic limits on consumption and enforce them collectively.

I am not offering a step-by-step proposal explaining how to transition from eight billion people consuming at an aggregate level that is unsustainable to a smaller population consuming at a sustainable level. I don't have such a plan. Given the immensity of the task and the contingencies of history, no one could pretend to have anything more than a rough idea of how to proceed. But ignoring a problem doesn't mean the problem resolves itself. Believing that supernatural forces will reorder the world is an abandonment of responsibility, as is betting on technological miracles. Beginning a difficult conversation about fewer and less is the first step toward fulfilling our responsibility to future generations.

LOOKING BACK

If we can't look for meaningful solutions from the right or the left, does it make sense to look back in time, not out of nostalgia but for useful insights? That depends on what one is seeking from the past.

For most of human history, people lived without the advanced technology and abundant energy that most of the contemporary world now takes for granted. Although humans have been drawing down the ecological capital of the planet since the invention of agriculture, that destruction has not been the same everywhere, and we can learn lessons by examining the past. One expert in biodiversity states:

> Indigenous peoples and other local communities, who might have lived in a region for thousands or hundreds of years, respectively, have long acted as foragers, growers and shapers of nature. In many parts of the world, the food production systems developed by such communities—from irrigated crops to agroforestry systems—have been the dominant food systems supporting regional economies, and feeding rural and urban areas alike.[205]

These lessons should lead us to sustainable agriculture, regenerative agriculture, agroecology—all terms for various approaches to growing food with few or no petrochemicals, turning away from high-tech pseudo-solutions. Many people are using ecological science and traditional wisdom to look for ways to feed ourselves without such intense stress on ecosystems. I support such projects, but with one reality check: No low-energy system can sustain eight billion people. Science can't create abundance out of nothing, and traditional systems of agriculture never supported today's population densities.

That is not to minimize the importance of scientific innovation nor to ignore indigenous insights. But we have to accept biophysical limits and be clear about history. Let's use as an example the continental United States, between the Mexican and Canadian borders. Many people rightly point to the more sustainable lifeways and economies of the varied indigenous North American cultures compared to Europeans' record of human exploitation and ecological degradation on the continent. There is, of course, considerable variety in indigenous North American societies, a product of the varied land and water resources of the continent. But without romanticizing those societies, we can say that the living arrangements developed in North America were more sustainable than those developed in Europe in the modern period.

Such comparisons are important, and the dominant culture should learn from any society that has lived successfully at lower levels of energy and resource consumption. But we must also recognize that those lifeways developed with much lower populations than today. The pre-contact population of the continental United States cannot be precisely determined, but estimates range from five to fifteen million. The current population on that same territory is more than three hundred million. For all of North and South America, the most common pre-contact population estimate is about sixty million; the current population is just over one billion. The traditional lifeways of indigenous America cannot support twenty times the population, even if amplified by the best of modern science.

Organisms tend to expand to the carrying capacity of the ecosystems in which they live, and humans are no different. The carrying capacity of the landscape for humans depends in part on how much energy humans can extract, which depends on technology. It's sensible to assume that indigenous societies expanded to that carrying capacity with their level of technology. The continental United States cannot support three hundred million people sustainably, nor can the Americas support one billion sustainably, without that additional energy. Less energy means fewer people.

None of these differences among societies is a function of differences in intelligence if we accept—as we should—the antiracist principle that we are one species. Indigenous Americans had not developed the plows that the Chinese and Europeans used to increase yields, nor did the Americas have draft animals that could pull them. Those realities limited how much could be produced. But there is no reason to believe that Chinese and Europeans invented plows because they were more intelligent than pre-contact Americans. Nor is there any reason to believe those pre-contact Americans understood how to make plows but chose not to do so. Because we are one species with the same capacities no matter where on Earth we have lived, the most plausible explanation for the development of different technologies in different places is geography, climate, and environmental conditions.

When presenting this perspective, I have been accused of trying to rationalize or excuse the barbarism of conquerors, past and present, which is not my goal. We are responsible for our actions today, which means pursuing policies that not only end the inequality and inequity established in the past but also try to rectify those injustices. My goal here is not rationalization but explanation, in the belief that deeper understanding makes it clearer what actions are necessary. That means taking seriously just how strong those temptations of dense energy have been and continue to be.

This does not mean individuals have no agency in the face of larger forces. After thousands of years of philosophical debate, people still seek a resolution of the free will/determinism debate, and I assume we will continue arguing about it until human extinction. (A sensible approach, I believe, is to assume that free will is an illusion and that we have no choice but to continue to act as if we have it.[206]) Whatever one's opinion, it's irresponsible to pretend there are not larger forces shaping human behavior, not only social but biological. For purposes of this inquiry, let's assume we have free will but that we have to contend with the temptations of dense energy. The human pattern of aggressive energy-seeking is relevant to whatever policies we adopt.

Among my left comrades, any talk of any level of determinism can be a conversation-stopper. Going back to *The Dawn of Everything*, a number of reviewers pointed out how Graeber and Wengrow play fast and loose with the often sketchy evidence from prehistory.[207] But even a reviewer who details those shortcomings of the book[208] praises the authors' "argument against historical determinism—against the alluring notion that what happened had to have happened."[209] This caricature of determinism as a claim that history is akin to a machine—humans on a conveyor belt without options—avoids rather than engages compelling arguments about how geography, climate, and environmental conditions have shaped history.[210] A sensible approach to determinism doesn't lead to predictions, which in human affairs are almost never of much value because we don't have the intellectual tools to identify all the relevant factors at play. But we should work to identify and understand, to the best of our ability, those history-shaping forces and recognize the limits of human agency.

This doesn't mean that the insights of many traditions can't help us find a path forward. Nor does it mean that we cannot use human creativity to solve problems, aware of the limitations and dangers of all technologies. We just have to commit to one simple idea: There are limits. Limits are not bad or good in moral terms, simply necessary. Any meaningful policy proposals should start with ideas for setting limits on our journey to fewer[211] and less.[212]

Those limits will have to be imposed collectively through rationing.[213] We cannot rely on individuals to do the right thing, because those temptations of dense energy can so easily overwhelm the best intentions of the most committed people. These collective limits won't come from "good" people lecturing "bad" people about how to be better. The only hope is, as many religious traditions remind us, to recognize we are all sinners (or at least, potential sinners if we get the chance). Yes, some people do more harm than others, and we should hold them accountable. Yes, some corporations are more responsible than others for ecosystem degradation, and we should hold them accountable. Yes, capitalism provides perverse incentives for ecological destruction, and we have to transcend this system. But in the end, the temptations of dense energy can't be wished away.

Nothing in this analysis suggests there's nothing that can be done. I'm not arguing for nihilism, but rather for a realistic assessment of our situation. Electric vehicles are a great example. Is it good to get vehicles that burn gasoline and diesel fuel off the road? Yes. Is replacing them with vehicles that run off batteries a good idea? Only if we ignore the human and environmental costs of mining the materials needed for such vehicles,[214] and only if we imagine those materials are unlimited.[215] Embracing EVs without considering the costs as well as the benefits is evidence not of bold thinking but of avoidance. The question is not only how we can eliminate internal combustion engines but also how we can dramatically reduce human travel.

We aren't helpless in these endeavors. When I made points like this in a presentation to a community group, someone in the audience suggested that I was overlooking valuable projects, such as organizing against militarism. The US military is not only a huge consumer of fossil fuels and other materials, but one of its primary missions is to ensure that the United States remains economically dominant so that consumption can continue and profits can be amassed. Ending US militarism, something

I've argued for and organized around for years, would be a major step toward sustainability. I agreed, but simply said that no combination of important goals like that would allow us to escape the core question: How do we get to fewer and less?

THE MORAL HIGH GROUND

My favorite sentence in *An Inconvenient Apocalypse* is, "The moral high ground is a dangerous place to stand, even when it's warranted," which Wes Jackson and I repeated several times in the book. That's true generally, but especially true in debates over environmental policy.

I repeat that warning for myself. We all are susceptible to arrogance. By "all," I do mean everyone. To warn against claiming that high ground is not to suggest that morality doesn't matter, that debating moral questions is irrelevant, or that no one is accountable for moral failure. Rather, I simply want to suggest that in political conflicts, we should remain open to alternative perspectives, just in case we are wrong, as everyone has been at various times in their lives and will be again. And even if we are right, we should recognize that being right doesn't make it obvious how to make things right in the world.

As an example, consider the executives from fossil fuel extraction corporations. Specifically, let's talk about ExxonMobil. It turns out that starting in the 1970s, Exxon (which merged with Mobil in 1999) was conducting research on how fossil fuels were warming the planet, even as it publicly cast doubt on climate science and opposed policies to reduce the use of those fuels.[216] Such behavior is unconscionable. Yes, everyone knows that oil companies make money selling oil, but knowledge of the catastrophic consequences of selling a product makes the company executives not simply negligent but guilty of crimes against people and planet.

Fair enough. Outrage is appropriate. Let's imagine that people are fired, fines are levied, charges are brought, and maybe even some people go to prison. Let's imagine that ExxonMobil is nationalized and a citizen board is appointed to chart a new course, redirecting company assets to renewable energy development. All that would be appropriate as well. But would the new citizen board members immediately end the extraction of oil? If they did, how would the oil-based infrastructure of the world operate? How would we collectively decide on prioritizing the use of remaining oil supplies to make sure that critical infrastructure operates during a transition? How would we prioritize ongoing energy uses, since no combination of renewable energy sources could replace the dense energy of fossil fuels?[217] Although renewable energy sources are expanding, and coming down in price, the United States still generates 79 percent of its energy from fossil fuels.[218] How would we adjudicate competing claims for the benefits of the remaining fossil fuels that we might decide can be responsibly used?

Nothing in this analysis excuses the behavior of Exxon and ExxonMobil executives. Nothing in this analysis suggests we shouldn't pursue civil and criminal penalties. This is just a warning about self-righteousness and over-simplification.

The moral high ground is a dangerous place to stand, even when it's warranted, because collectively we face hard choices that not only have no easy answers but may not have answers at all, at least answers that we know how to find.

For emphasis, I will repeat myself: There likely are no solutions to the multiple cascading crises of our moment in history, if by solutions we mean ways to sustain eight billion people on Earth, let alone eight billion people with a significant number of them continuing to live in high-energy/high-technology societies. Meaningful discussion of solutions has to start with embracing limits and moving toward fewer and less.

I realize this likely sounds callous to people who have so little in today's profoundly immoral division of wealth and power. It will sound cruel to people who live with the most destructive consequences of modern industrial society. Working and poor people—disproportionately black and brown in the United States, and non-white throughout the Global South—suffer in ways I do not. I am not poor. I am not a victim of environmental racism, the dumping of the worst ecological problems on those with the least responsibility for generating the waste. If readers conclude that I'm a jerk for pushing this analysis, I certainly understand. But that doesn't make the analysis unsound. The question isn't whether

I have enormous privilege—obviously, I do. The question isn't whether those without my privilege might bristle at this conclusion—I suspect some will. The question is, what is the reality we face?

Many people feel systems unraveling, and many people are scared. I believe systems are unraveling, and I am scared.

I believe in persevering, even in the face of the fear that we aren't up to the task, individually and collectively. That's likely to be more productive if we can give up hubris, individually and collectively. This hubris, as many a storyteller over the millennia has suggested, may be our fatal flaw, not just as individuals but collectively. But humility is always available to us.

Our self-naming offers a hint at which way we should turn. Our genus, *Homo* (Latin for "human being") began 2.5 million years ago with *Homo habilis*, which is usually translated as "handy" or "skillful." We named ourselves *Homo sapiens*, the "wise" ones.

Imagine asking two people how to describe themselves. One says, "I'm pretty handy." The other declares, "I am wise." Who would you rather hang out with? It's not that we aren't capable of wisdom, only that in a fewer-and-less future, we're going to have to realize the limits of the types of "wisdom" that have landed us in this predicament and learn to be a lot handier.

Conclusion:
Where Are We Going?

This book's epigraph comes from John Stuart Mill's[219] classic *On Liberty*, first published in 1859. To bring the themes of this book together, I want to highlight the arguments he made for an expansive conception of freedom of speech.

First, an opinion that is silenced by power may be the truth, and suppression of the truth is bad news, at least for those who want to find the truth. Second, even if the silenced opinion is in some sense wrong, it could contain part of the truth; suppression is a bad outcome in that case as well. Third, even if a silenced opinion is completely wrong and the conventional wisdom contains the whole truth, that truth will become like a prejudice if not contested, "preventing the growth of any real and heartfelt conviction from reason or personal experience."[220] All these outcomes are bad, not only for the individuals silenced but for society as a whole. Ever since I read the book nearly four decades ago, I have liked the phrase he uses in making that third argument, "dead dogma":

> However unwillingly a person who has a strong opinion may admit the possibility that his opinion may be false, he ought to be moved by the consideration that, however true it may be, if it is not fully, frequently, and fearlessly discussed, it will be held as a dead dogma, not a living truth.[221]

No one is likely to admit they prefer "dead dogma." But various dogmas—defined as claims, religious or secular, that are taken to be true without sufficient justification—have many fans. People have varying levels of tolerance for uncertainty and varying levels of interest in wrestling with the unexplainable complexity of the world. Scientific skepticism—questioning any claim that lacks empirical validation—isn't the preferred approach for everyone. Many people seek certainty in an uncertain world. Dogma can seem reassuring.

Though it sounds a bit haughty, I will state my preference for living truths. My goal in this book has been to demonstrate why we should fully, frequently, and fearlessly (what a nice alliterative list of three) discuss matters of public concern, even when it puts us at odds with political opponents, and even more so when it puts us at odds with political allies. We need to think freely, recognizing that speaking responsibly about our thoughts will lead to disagreement, debate, and discomfort. To turn away from that discomfort makes it impossible to live authentically.

Here's a bit of discomfort about Mill himself: He supported freedom of expression and women's rights, but he also embraced British imperialism, worked for the British East India Company, and held paternalistic views about non-Western peoples. Critics have pointed out that his defense of liberty was not as expansive as it could have been. A more charitable scholar suggests that, over time, Mill saw the problems of British rule and adopted a "melancholic colonialism" that was "marked by anxiety, even despondency, about the direction of (colonial) history," though he continued to believe that an ideal colonialism could provide universal benefits such as civilization, peace, and prosperity.[222]

I find it hard to feel too bad for Mill and his melancholy, but whatever the scope and trajectory of his imperialist ideology, Mill doesn't need to be a secular saint for us to appreciate his philosophical insights. If we can learn only from those who have perfect records on all moral questions, the world would have no teachers. As I have stressed, humility is appropriate for everyone. If Mill were alive today, I suspect he would agree with that. If he didn't, he surely would after reading this book. (I feel the need to point out that was a joke, which means I'm not nearly as clever a writer as I want to be.)

Even if Mill were to come back to life and proclaim me a dunce, I think he would be thoughtful in his assessment of my failures, because he argued for:

> giving merited honor to everyone, whatever opinion he may hold, who has calmness to see and honesty to state what his opponents and their opinions really are, exaggerating nothing to their discredit, keeping nothing back which tells, or can be supposed to tell, in their favor. This is the real morality of public discussion.[223]

Even though I have presented arguments in a fashion that some might find to be aggressive, I think I have lived up to that standard. But does any of it matter? Here's one more aspect of Mill's analysis that I think is important for our times: his realistic assessment of the platitude that truth always prevails:

> It is a piece of idle sentimentality that truth, merely as truth, has any inherent power denied to error, of prevailing against the dungeon and the stake. Men are not more zealous for truth than they often are for error, and a sufficient application of legal or even of social penalties will generally succeed in stopping the propagation of either.[224]

Mill wrote in the nineteenth century, but my experience that validates these lessons came in the twenty-first. I'll describe two episodes from my life in which thinking, speaking, and acting led to conflict—with people in authority in one case and with comrades in another. I've never faced the dungeon or the stake, or anything close to those punishments, for which I'm grateful. But I have seen how social penalties can be effective in silencing people, as illustrated by the censure from my bosses because of writing I did after the terrorist attacks of September 11, 2001, and the shunning that came after my critique of the ideology of transgenderism. In both cases, censure and shunning didn't much change my behavior but did have an effect on choices that others made.

9/11 AND THE FAILURE OF A UNIVERSITY

One of the most important decisions a country can make is the choice to go to war. In a healthy democratic culture, that decision should be thoroughly debated before political leaders deploy troops in battle. But within hours after the 9/11 attacks, politicians of both parties were climbing over each other to get to microphones to call for a military response.

I spent most of that day in my office watching the news coverage while trying to reach friends in New York to make sure they were safe. My memory of the day is blurry, but I remember clearly that by mid-afternoon—before anyone even had a clear understanding of the details of the events—it seemed inevitable that the United States would bomb someone, somewhere in retaliation. Whether it would be legal or sensible was irrelevant—politicians were preparing to use the terrorist attacks to justify war. By the end of that day, I had written the first of many articles sharply criticizing US foreign policy and arguing strongly against going to war.[225]

Not everyone agreed with me. For weeks, my voicemail and inbox were filled with critics who described me as a coward, a traitor, unpatriotic, and/or unmanly. (The most revealing, in a psychological sense, were the messages from men who imagined the sexual punishment I deserved, including being raped by Osama bin Laden.) After that article ran in the state's largest newspaper and became a topic on conservative talk radio, people began calling for the university to fire me. Within two weeks, the president of the University of Texas at Austin responded publicly, calling me "misguided" and describing me as "an undiluted fountain of foolishness."[226] (He was a chemist, not a poet.) Other university officials added their own denunciations, some of which were forwarded to me, but none of my bosses confronted me directly. Because I was a tenured professor with considerable job protection, none of them moved to fire me.

The criticism continued for a few months, but I continued to write and speak out. At the time, I was already a part of a small national network opposing US militarism, and the support of people in that movement sustained me. Locally, we formed the group Austin Against

War to organize protests and do political outreach. Around the country and throughout the world, many people defied the jingoist rhetoric and challenged that militarism.

The university president's statement had no effect on my activity, but it was effective in a larger sense. Many UT faculty members shared my views, yet only a handful joined the initial organizing efforts, I assume at least in part because of fear of being targeted as I had been. One untenured professor I knew stopped speaking out against militarism after his dean told him that continuing to circulate critical writing would almost certainly cost him his job, and I assume others made similar choices. Several graduate students from other countries told me they wanted to get involved in antiwar organizing but were afraid it could lead to the US government revoking their visas. Faculty colleagues with lawful permanent resident status who were from Muslim-majority countries on a special-registration list created the following year (the National Security Entry-Exit Registration System) told me they feared that the government would revoke their green cards even for trivial errors in record-keeping. The threat of legal action, fears about losing jobs, and peer pressure were enough to undermine a robust debate on my campus, though student activists created as much space as they could.

The United States invaded Afghanistan with little domestic or international opposition beyond the small antiwar groups and pacifists. The Bush administration's weak case for invading Iraq sparked more domestic and international opposition, leading to the world's largest coordinated day of political protest on February 15, 2003, when millions of people unsuccessfully sought to stop the pending invasion. Soon it was clear that the antiwar movement's analysis had been sound, as the disastrous consequences of those ill-advised invasions began to be measured in hundreds of thousands of deaths, trillions of dollars, and destabilized societies in the Middle East and Central Asia.[227]

Protected by tenure, I continued teaching at UT until retirement in 2018. That was positive for me, but it does not change the fact that my university failed in its obligation to foster the conversation that citizens in a democratic society needed at a crucial moment in history. Throughout that period, I argued not only that I had a right to speak out but that the university had a duty to provide a forum to make use of the expertise of the faculty and engage the community. In debates over going to war, which understandably generate strong emotions, evidence and logic are crucial, and universities have valuable resources to offer. The dominant culture needed, and still needs, to engage the evidence and logic presented by critics of US imperial foreign policy and militarism.

TRANSGENDERISM AND THE FAILURE OF THE LEFT

In Chapter 5, I detailed my critique of the ideology of the transgender movement and what I believe is the failure of liberal/progressive/left people and organizations to engage with radical feminist critiques of patriarchy. I want to say a bit more about how that affected my life and how it has affected intellectual life on the left.

I knew the potential consequences when in 2014 I wrote my first article outlining an analysis rooted in the radical feminist perspective on transgenderism,[228] but feminist colleagues had challenged me to get off the sidelines in the debate, and I knew they were right. Later that year, a local left/anarchist bookstore that I had long supported sent an email blast (without speaking to me first) announcing that it was severing all ties with me.[229] Trans activists came to some of my public lectures on feminist topics to protest or try to shout me down, even though the talks weren't about transgenderism.[230] Several groups that had invited me to speak about such topics as the ecological crisis withdrew invitations after receiving complaints. And, of course, I can't know how many people who might have wanted to include me in an activity declined to invite me just to avoid hassles.

No person or organization has an obligation to associate with me, of course. The unfortunate aspect of all this was that none of the organizations or people who shunned or de-platformed me ever explained why my writing was unacceptable, beyond repeating accusations of transphobia. I was denounced for holding views that were asserted to be unacceptable, though no coherent argument to support that denunciation was ever presented to me.

This pattern continued for the remainder of my time at the University of Texas and in Austin, as many friends and political allies with whom I had worked on a variety of education and organizing projects avoided me. After the 2016 presidential election, I was part of a group that organized a teach-in on the political consequences of Donald Trump's presidency. By that time, I knew my role should be behind the scenes, to avoid everyone's work being derailed by an objection to my involvement. I had already received enough criticism to know that if I were one of the speakers, trans activists might protest. So, I handled catering and publicity, out of public view, except that the publicity material included my name and email address. That was enough to generate at least one complaint to the university, from someone who said he wouldn't feel safe attending, knowing that I was involved in any way.

It turned out that was the last collective organizing project I was part of, either at UT or with liberal/progressive/left organizations in Austin. When I talked with people about collaborating on education events that in previous years they would have wanted to be involved in, they told me my trans writing made it impossible. More common was silence; people I had worked with in the past simply stopped returning emails or phone messages. I continued to work on projects, either alone or with one trusted friend who shared my analysis, but I was no longer welcome in most left circles.

I also had a number of friends and university colleagues who agreed with my critique, but would acknowledge that position only when speaking privately. These were not shy people who were afraid of public conversation about contentious issues in general. But they had observed the backlash to any challenge to the liberal/progressive/left orthodoxy on transgenderism and wanted to avoid being attacked. I never held that against anyone; we all make strategic decisions about what political battles we want to fight.

The strangest experiences came with a few friends who seemed afraid to talk even privately, always steering conversations away from the subject. In two cases, I never really understood what my friends thought about the issue. Why the hesitancy to discuss something that was so much a part of the public debate about sex/gender justice, which they both cared about deeply, even when talking in private? I can think of two reasons. They may not have trusted me to keep their remarks confidential, but in both cases I had kept confidences before and they had no reason to doubt me. The more plausible explanation is that they didn't want to consider reasons to challenge the liberal position that was dogma in their institutions. One of them read my 2017 book, *The End of Patriarchy*, and wrote me to say he thought that the chapter on transgenderism was "a great expansion of your original argument. I just don't like it, even though it appears to be perfectly logical." He later told me that he found conversation about the subject "unsettling," and I honored his request that we not discuss it further.

While these experiences were at times stressful and generally unpleasant, women who have challenged the transgender-industrial complex tend to fare much worse.[231] I never lost a job[232] and have never been physically attacked.[233] I lost some friends and missed out on organizing efforts to which I think I could have contributed, but I had other friends to rely on and always found a way to continue doing meaningful political work.

Just as in the 9/11 example, my experience isn't a story of how my freedom of expression was constrained. No governmental agency shut me down, and the rejection didn't stop me from writing or speaking out. Many other radical feminists continue to write and speak, as well. But many more people have either muted themselves or been driven out of organizations. It's hard to imagine how we will deepen our understanding of a subject as complex as transgenderism if people making reasonable arguments that challenge the current liberal dogma are constantly attacked.

One last personal reflection. My biggest frustration is when trans activists tell me that my work is evidence of transphobia. Stonewall, a prominent UK LGBTQ+ organization, defines transphobia as the "fear or dislike of someone based on the fact they are trans, including denying their gender identity or refusing to accept it."[234] I do not fear or dislike people who identify as transgender, and I don't deny their own sense of their identity. Offering an alternative explanation of an experience is not refusing to accept the experience.

This is not merely an academic question for me. As a child, I was short, skinny, effeminate, and late to hit puberty—I was the smallest boy in my class and lived with a constant fear of being targeted by other boys. I also grew up in an abusive household that made impossible any semblance of "normal" development. Until the age of thirty, I had no way to make sense of that experience and assumed I was just an oddball. When I began reading feminism, especially the radical feminist writers whom I found most compelling, I realized that parts of my experience were common in patriarchy. I had suffered in the way many boys in a patriarchal society suffer, and as a man I had sought to escape that suffering by conforming to patriarchal norms of masculinity. Feminism offered a way out of that trap.

I have empathy for people who don't fit conventional categories and face ridicule or violence for being different, in part because I have experienced those struggles and threats. I have tried to present arguments based on credible evidence and sound logic, but underneath those intellectual positions are my own struggle, pain, and grief, which I think has sensitized me to the struggle, pain, and grief of others. But emotions are by themselves not an argument. Evidence and logic matter. The transgender movement needs to engage the evidence and logic presented by radical feminism.

CONSISTENCY IS NOT FOOLISH

A few years ago, I published an essay arguing that my left comrades were inconsistent when it came to the analysis of some sex/gender issues,[235] a problem I mentioned in Chapter 1. A hallmark of left analysis is to look first at systems and structures of power rather than at individual choices within existing institutions. On the left, the focus is on capitalism-the-system, not the choices that individuals make within capitalism. There are workers in capitalist firms who embrace the boss, believe that hard work is rewarded fairly, and reject labor unions as interference in their freedom to choose. But that doesn't mean capitalism's critics are wrong. The same goes for white supremacy. There are people of color who reject the critique of systemic and structural racism, but that doesn't negate analyses of white supremacy that focus on institutions.

This is one example of how liberals and leftists tend to be different. One key way that leftists distinguish themselves from liberals is the left's goal of replacing exploitative and oppressive systems rather than merely improving the lot of people within such systems. Liberals want to tinker with capitalism to make it fairer. Leftists want to replace capitalism with some form of socialism. Liberals want the United States to practice a kinder-and-gentler domination around the globe. Leftists want to end imperialism.

But many leftists become liberals when it come to the sexual-exploitation industries, the term I use for pornography, prostitution, stripping, massage parlors, and other ways that men routinely buy and sell objectified female bodies for sexual pleasure. The same is true in the case of transgender ideology—people on the left routinely embrace a liberal position on these issues, focusing on maximizing personal choice rather than on the oppressive system of institutionalized male dominance and its gender norms.

After giving a presentation a few years ago in which I mentioned this, I spoke with a leftie from the audience, who seemed sympathetic to my argument but unwilling to break with his political community. He defended his comrades by offering what likely is the most common quotation on the subject of consistency, from Ralph Waldo Emerson's essay "Self-Reliance": "A foolish consistency is the hobgoblin of little minds, adored by little statesmen and philosophers and divines."[236] He actually misquoted Emerson, which is also common, by rendering it as "Consistency is the hobgoblin of little minds."

I responded that Emerson wasn't mocking consistency in the application of principles but rather was suggesting that seeking a "foolish consistency" in opinion over time was dangerous. We may change our minds because conditions change, or we acquire new knowledge, or we rethink our assumptions. In such cases, changing our minds is sensible. Holding onto a false belief because we had previously endorsed it would, indeed, be foolish. Applying a principle in a consistent manner not only isn't foolish, but is essential to critical thinking.

Later I was discussing this difference with a friend who is both a leftist and a scientist, and I suggested that on the left we need to strive for consistency in standards for evaluating evidence. He suggested I might be expecting too much from people in political life. In a scientific discipline, he said, there are relatively clear protocols for inquiry that make it easier for that kind of consistency, but in politics these protocols aren't as well established. Fair enough, but I wasn't demanding the same rigor in everyday political discussions that is the standard in a laboratory (acknowledging that standards are not met perfectly in the lab). In our email exchange, I elaborated:

> I'm talking about a general intellectual standard that says principles should be applied uniformly to all relevant cases. I don't think that takes a specific commitment to a scientific discipline but rather a commitment to intellectual honesty. So, if Principle A applies to Case X, and Case Y is the same in all relevant features to Case X, then Principle A should apply to Case Y. I can't imagine anyone disputing that standard. If a political movement applies that standard in most cases, but then abandons it in another case, that's what I mean by inconsistency. And I'm saying we should all strive for that consistency, based on a good-faith commitment to shared intellectual standards.

My embrace of a principled consistency doesn't guarantee I'm right about everything. I may have started out with the wrong assumptions or I may be overlooking important evidence. If I am misguided in any analysis, my only request is that people who disagree explain why they reject my argument rather than merely denounce me or my position. After 9/11, my critics were quick to denounce and often unwilling to engage. In the transgender debate, I've had the same experience.

For emphasis: By offering examples of what I believe to be failures of my critics from both the right and left, I'm not suggesting that I occupy some sensible centrist position that allows me to see everyone's errors. I'm on the political left, and I don't assume I'm infallible. If I spend more time critiquing the left, it's because I want to contribute to strengthening left analyses. Especially when caught up in what feel like crucial political struggles, it's easy for any individual or group of people to see the flaws in the ideology and arguments of opponents and avoid one's own failures. One need not be a Christian to appreciate this warning about hypocrisy:

> "Why do you look at the speck of sawdust in your brother's eye and pay no attention to the plank in your own eye? How can you say to your brother, 'Brother, let me take the speck out of your eye,' when you yourself fail to see the plank in your own eye? You hypocrite, first take the plank out of your eye, and then you will see clearly to remove the speck from your brother's eye." (Luke 6:41–42)

TRUTH IN CHAPTER TITLES: A CONFESSION

I should confess that I titled this concluding chapter "Where Are We Going?" even though I have no idea how to answer the question. It just sounded like a good pairing with an introductory chapter titled "Where I'm Coming From." Calling this concluding section "I Have No Idea How to Make Sense of Much of Anything Going on These Days" would have been more honest but less elegant.

I've already expressed my reluctance to make predictions, which is intensified by my belief that the "cascading" part of today's multiple cascading crises makes it impossible to offer anything more than a general guess at the specifics of the crises that lie ahead. Human societies have made a mess before, but the impossible-to-predict unfolding of today's global ecological crises is unprecedented. I also have no prediction on the direction of the political and social polarization of the moment.

Given all this uncertainty, I think we should assume that the warnings of rapid ecological collapse are justified and plan for that future of fewer and less, which is going to require greater collaboration across ideological lines.

When sorting through these questions, I often find myself thinking of my late friend Jim Koplin. I've told his story at length in another book,[237] but what is on my mind these days are the final years of Jim's life. He remained committed to radical feminism, antiracist organizing, and left politics. But as he got older, he spent less time on conventional political activity and more time building relationships in his community. Rather than launch into a lecture, he waited for people to express interest in political issues and then would gently suggest a book to read or an idea to consider. Only after getting to know someone would he offer judgments, and even then, he had a way of arguing without being judgmental. Only with his closest friends would he be blunt, sometimes even harsh, when he thought we were wrong.

As readers can see, I have a hard time following Jim's example. I am more combative than he was, though as I get older I no longer seek out that combat as enthusiastically as I once did. But following Jim's lead, my goal in this book is not to suggest that everyone should share my exact approach to intellectual life, let alone reach the political conclusions I have reached. I am not saying "think like me." Instead, I want to model a way to think that neither pretends to be solitary nor automatically conforms to the expectations of a group. If we embrace our collective life and remain true to our own thoughts, inevitably we will have to confront colleagues when we believe them to be wrong. That's what Karl Marx meant, I think, when he called for a "ruthless criticism."

I have cited these lines from Marx often, partly for strategic reasons. It annoys conservatives to read Marx quoted in a way that they have a hard time disagreeing with, and my left comrades have a hard time rejecting Marx even if they don't like the point I'm trying to make. So, here's what Marx wrote about that need for humility as well as the obligation to confront both opponents and ourselves, written in 1843 when he was twenty-five years old, in a letter to a friend:

> But, if constructing the future and settling everything for all times are not our affair, it is all the more clear what we have to accomplish at present: I am referring to ruthless criticism of all that exists, ruthless both in the sense of not being afraid of the results it arrives at and in the sense of being just as little afraid of conflict with the powers that be.[238]

Confronting the powers that be can be difficult, especially when those powers are cruel and brutal, as they routinely have been throughout history. We rightly honor those who didn't back down and often suffered for their courage. But it also takes courage not to be afraid of the results, especially when those results leave us feeling isolated from our communities.

I don't know where *we* are going, toward chaos or community, to borrow from Martin Luther King Jr., one of the many who paid the ultimate price for that confrontation.[239] My assumption is that there is considerable chaos ahead, which makes forming and strengthening real communities today all the more crucial.

It's possible that in chaotic times, people will abandon rigid ideologies and find new ways to work with everyone in their communities to enhance survival and make possible a more decent human future. It's also possible that when the chaos intensifies, people's commitment to ideologies will intensify and it will become more difficult to be humane to each other. And it's possible, as some evolutionary biologists have speculated, that human intelligence is a lethal mutation—that we are smart enough to destroy ourselves and not wise enough to keep ourselves from doing it.

I don't know where we are going, and I have no reason to expect that anyone else has a better grasp on the future than I do. My concluding thoughts are inadequate to the task in front of us, as anyone's conclusions are bound to be.

With that caveat, here are a few guidelines I feel confident in proposing.

- Like everyone, I see the world through my ideologies, the frameworks of understanding that everyone uses to organize the complexity of the world. But I can strive to avoid becoming an ideologue, someone who doubles down on ideology when that framework clashes with material realities.
- Our chances of a humane future are diminished if we prefer denial and delusion to facing harsh realities. Denying the scope of problems and constructing delusional plans will only intensify human suffering and ecological degradation.

- To test our ideologies and resist the temptation to avoid unpleasant realities, we should not dismiss the ideas that challenge us nor denounce those who hold those ideas without taking seriously the possibility that we have something to learn.

That's my program: ideological but not an ideologue, rejecting denial and delusion, refusing to dismiss or denounce. It may not seem like an ambitious program, but in my experience, it is difficult to live up to, even for those with the best intentions.

I have no advice on how to live that program, except to surround oneself with people who have the same goal. How we manage to live up to our own expectations is increasingly a mystery to me, which is captured in a story my friend Wes Jackson tells.

"IT WASN'T ME"

Wes ran track in high school and college and later coached at both levels. In his long career in education and environmental organizing, he traveled widely and met more than his share of interesting and famous people. But he said the only time he felt like a groupie is when he met famous track stars. Among his favorite moments was a conversation with Billy Mills, the underdog runner who won the 10,000 meters at the 1964 Tokyo Olympics, one of the most thrilling races in Olympic history.

At a gathering of University of Kansas track alumni, Wes got a chance to sit with Mills, who was characteristically modest about his achievement. Wes tells the story in his book *Hogs Are Up*:

> [Mills's] reply to my praise, my admiration, my recounting moments within the race and his strong sprint across the finish line was simply this: "Well, Wes, it wasn't me." This was a sacred moment for me, and I did not ask, "What do you mean?" or "How so?" I wasn't sure what he meant, but it didn't seem like my place to probe further.[240]

When Wes first told me the story several years ago, I chastised him for not asking Mills to explain what he meant by "It wasn't me," suggesting that he missed a chance to go deeper with Mills. Was Mills referring to the support he got from his team and coach? From his community? From a spiritual source? Or, did he just mean that we never really know why things happen the way they do, and it's best to be humble?

As time has gone by, I have grown to appreciate Wes's decision not to probe, at least in part because I have recognized my own inability to understand my own work and life (which includes no Olympic medals or significant honors). When I think of anything I've accomplished, I'm hard-pressed to explain how it came to be. The older I get, the more "It wasn't me" seems the right answer, in the sense that outcomes in our lives are hard to explain. We should take responsibility for our failures, even though our mistakes are usually at least in part a shared failure with others. But when we succeed, it's best to decline credit.

I am responsible for my mistakes, but my successes belong to the collective. I know that's illogical. Given my emphasis on logical arguments throughout this book, I am chuckling at myself for ending on this note. If we think collectively, and if we are all subject to forces we cannot control, and if free will itself might be an illusion—then whether I'm right or wrong, it's not solely mine to claim. But that's the only way I know how to get through the world today.

If there are errors in this book, they are mine.

If there is any value in this book, it wasn't me.

Endnotes

A note on sources: I have used a variety of sources—including scholarly journals, professional journalism, and specialty publications—to support my arguments. As often as possible, I have used sources that are available online, preferably without a paywall, to make it easier for readers to check the accuracy of my claims.

INTRODUCTION:
WHERE I'M COMING FROM

1   Dan M. Kahan et al., "Culture and Identity-Protective Cognition: Explaining the White-Male Effect in Risk Perception," *Journal of Empirical Legal Studies* 4, no. 3 (November 2007): 465-505, https://papers.ssrn.com/sol3/papers.cfm?abstract_id=995634.

2   Dan M. Kahan, Hank Jenkins-Smith, and Donald Braman, "Cultural Cognition of Scientific Consensus," *Journal of Risk Research* 14 (2011): 147-74, https://papers.ssrn.com/sol3/papers.cfm?abstract_id=3334657.

3   Noam Chomsky, Ian Roberts, and Jeffrey Watumull, "The False Promise of ChatGPT," *New York Times*, March 8, 2023, https://www.nytimes.com/2023/03/08/opinion/noam-chomsky-chatgpt-ai.html.

4   "Abe Osheroff: On the Joys and Risks of Living in the Empire," interview by Robert Jensen, 2005, https://robertwjensen.org/wp-content/uploads/2015/12/Abe-Osheroff-interview-by-Robert-Jensen.pdf.

5   *Abe Osheroff: One Foot in the Grave, the Other Still Dancing,*
       directed by Nadeem Uddin (Northampton, MA: Media Education
       Foundation, 2009), https://www.kanopy.com/en/product/
       abe-osheroff-one-foot-grave-other-still-da.

6   My reflections on Jim, along with his obituary and photos, are online at
       https://robertwjensen.org/category/jim-koplin/.

7   Wes Jackson and Robert Jensen, *An Inconvenient Apocalypse: Environmental
       Collapse, Climate Crisis, and the Fate of Humanity* (South Bend, IN: University
       of Notre Dame Press, 2022).

8   Robert Jensen, *Plain Radical: Living, Loving, and Learning to Leave the
       Planet Gracefully* (Berkeley, CA: Counterpoint/Soft Skull, 2015), 124.

9   Michael Walzer, *The Struggle for a Decent Politics: On "Liberal" as an
       Adjective* (New Haven, CT: Yale University Press, 2023), 3.

10   Kelefa Sanneh, "How Christian Is Christian Nationalism?"
       The New Yorker, March 27, 2023, https://www.newyorker.com/
       magazine/2023/04/03/how-christian-is-christian-nationalism;
       Kristin Du Mez, "A Virtual Roundtable on the Threat of Christian
       Nationalism," Du Mez CONNECTIONS, February 15, 2023,
       https://kristindumez.substack.com/p/a-virtual-roundtable-on-the-threat.

CHAPTER 1:
STEPPING UP: CONTEMPORARY CONTROVERSIES

11   Sixth Assessment Report, Climate Change 2023, Intergovernmental Panel
       on Climate Change, https://www.ipcc.ch/report/ar6/syr/.

12   Pasquale Borrelli et al., "An Assessment of the Global Impact of 21st
       Century Land Use Change on Soil Erosion," *Nature Communications* 8, no.
       2013 (2017), https://www.nature.com/articles/s41467-017-02142-7.

13   Linn Perrson et al., "Outside the Safe Operating Space of the Planetary
       Boundary for Novel Entities," *Environmental Science & Technology* 56, no. 3
       (2022): 1510–1521, https://pubs.acs.org/doi/10.1021/acs.est.1c04158.

14   "What Are the Extent and Causes of Biodiversity Loss?" Grantham
       Research Institute on Climate Change and the Environment,
       December 2, 2022, https://www.lse.ac.uk/granthaminstitute/explainers/
       what-are-the-extent-and-causes-of-biodiversity-loss/.

15   Recent examples are the Forward Party, the Renew America Movement, and the Serve America Movement, which in 2022 announced they would merge into a single political party called Forward, https://fwdtogether.org/. The No Labels political organization describes itself as "the voice for the great American majority who increasingly feel politically homeless" and highlights its bipartisan approach, https://www.nolabels.org/why.

16   Ibram X. Kendi, "The Crisis of the Intellectuals," *The Atlantic*, March 23, 2023, https://www.theatlantic.com/ideas/archive/2023/03/intellectualism-crisis-american-racism/673480/.

17   Geoffrey Hughes, *Political Correctness: A History of Semantics and Culture* (Malden, MA: Wiley-Blackwell, 2010).

18   James Davison Hunter, *Culture Wars: The Struggle to Define America* (New York: Basic Books, 1991).

19   Lead Belly, "Scottsboro Boys" (*Lead Belly: The Smithsonian Folkways Collection*, 2015), https://www.youtube.com/watch?v=VrXfkPViFIE.

20   Michael Harriot, "Weaponizing 'Woke': A Brief History of White Definitions," The Root, November 12, 2021, https://www.theroot.com/weaponizing-woke-an-brief-history-of-white-definitions-1848031729; Aja Romano, "A History of 'Wokeness,'" Vox, Oct 9, 2020, https://www.vox.com/culture/21437879/stay-woke-wokeness-history-origin-evolution-controversy.

21   Ralph Benko, "Let the Right Take Heart: 'Woke' Is Doing the Left In," Newsmax, July 18, 2022, https://www.newsmax.com/ralphbenko/alinsky-christianity-goldwater/2022/07/18/id/1079276/.

22   Tadeg Quillien, "Is Virtue Signalling a Vice?" Aeon, April 4, 2022, https://aeon.co/essays/why-virtue-signalling-is-not-just-a-vice-but-an-evolved-tool.

23   Maurice Mitchell, "Building Resilient Organizations: Toward Joy and Durable Power in a Time of Crisis," Convergence, November 29, 2022, https://convergencemag.com/articles/building-resilient-organizations-toward-joy-and-durable-power-in-a-time-of-crisis/.

24   Lulu Garcia-Navarro, "The Left Is Eating Itself," *New York Times*, January 26, 2023, https://www.nytimes.com/2023/01/26/opinion/the-left-purity-politics.html.

25   Aditya Aladangady and Akila Forde, "Wealth Inequality and the Racial Wealth Gap," Federal Reserve System, FEDS Notes, October 22, 2021, https://www.federalreserve.gov/econres/notes/feds-notes/wealth-inequality-and-the-racial-wealth-gap-20211022.html.

26   Vincent Lloyd, "A Black Professor Trapped in Anti-Racist Hell," *Compact Magazine*, February 10, 2023, https://compactmag.com/article/a-black-professor-trapped-in-anti-racist-hell.

27   Conor Friedersdorf, "An Anti-Racist Professor Faces 'Toxicity on the Left Today,'" *The Atlantic*, February 17, 2023, https://www.theatlantic.com/ideas/archive/2023/02/villanova-professor-vincent-lloyd-anti-racism-conversation/673079/.

28   Loretta J. Ross, "Don't Call People Out—Call Them In," filmed in Monterey, CA, August 2021, TED video, 14:14, https://www.ted.com/speakers/loretta_j_ross; Jessica Bennett, "What if Instead of Calling People Out, We Called Them In?" *New York Times*, November 19, 2020, https://www.nytimes.com/2020/11/19/style/loretta-ross-smith-college-cancel-culture.html; Loretta Ross, "I'm a Black Feminist. I Think Call-Out Culture Is Toxic," *New York Times*, August 17, 2019, https://www.nytimes.com/2019/08/17/opinion/sunday/cancel-culture-call-out.html.

29   For examples of how such a decision hinges on context, see Jack Stripling, "The Professor Is Canceled. Now What?" *Washington Post*, June 21, 2023, https://www.washingtonpost.com/education/2023/06/21/college-professors-fired-cancel-culture/; Vimal Patel, "UPenn Accuses a Law Professor of Racist Statements. Should She Be Fired?" *New York Times*, March 13, 2023, https://www.nytimes.com/2023/03/13/us/upenn-law-professor-racism-freedom-speech.html.

30   "White Privilege Shapes the U.S.," *Baltimore Sun*, July 19, 1998, C-1, https://www.baltimoresun.com/news/bs-xpm-1998-07-19-1998200115-story.html.

31   Robert Jensen, *The Heart of Whiteness: Confronting Race, Racism and White Privilege* (San Francisco: City Lights Books, 2005).

32   Robert Jensen, *The End of Patriarchy: Radical Feminism for Men* (North Melbourne, Australia: Spinifex Press, 2017).

CHAPTER 2:
STEPPING BACK: THINKING

33 Debbie Kasper, *Beyond the Knowledge Crisis: A Synthesis Framework for Socio-Environmental Studies and Guide to Social Change* (Cham, Switzerland: Palgrave Macmillan/Springer Nature, 2021), 25.

34 *Plain Radical*, 42.

35 Dan M. Kahan et al., "Science Curiosity and Political Information Processing," *Political Psychology* (Supplement: Advances in Political Psychology) 38, no. S1 (2017): 179–199, https://doi.org/10.1111/pops.12396.

36 Julia Galef, *The Scout Mindset: Why Some People See Things Clearly and Others Don't* (New York: Portfolio/Penguin, 2021).

37 For a review, see Jonathan Jenkins Ichikawa and Matthias Steup, "The Analysis of Knowledge," in *The Stanford Encyclopedia of Philosophy*, ed. Edward N. Zalta (Summer 2018 edition), https://plato.stanford.edu/archives/sum2018/entries/knowledge-analysis/.

38 James R. Steiner-Dillon, "Sticking Points: Epistemic Pluralism in Legal Challenges to Mandatory Vaccination Policies," *University of Cincinnati Law Review* 88 (2019): 169–237.

39 Scott Nearing, *The Making of a Radical: A Political Autobiography* (White River Junction, VT: Chelsea Green Publishing, 2000), 56.

40 Karin Gwinn Wilkins, *Questioning Numbers: How to Read and Critique Research* (New York: Oxford University Press, 2011), 2–3.

41 Susann Wagenknecht, *A Social Epistemology of Research Groups: Collaboration in Scientific Practice* (London: Palgrave Macmillan, 2016), 109.

42 From the Ms. Magazine Project on Campus Sexual Assault, summarized in Mary P. Koss, "Hidden Rape: Sexual Aggression and Victimization in a National Sample of Students in Higher Education," in ed. Ann Wolbert Burgess, *Rape and Sexual Assault II* (New York: Garland, 1988), 3–25.

43 Belinda-Rose Young et al., "Sexual Coercion Practices Among Undergraduate Male Recreational Athletes, Intercollegiate Athletes, and Non-Athletes," *Violence Against Women* 23, no. 7 (2017): 795–812, https://journals.sagepub.com/doi/abs/10.1177/1077801216651339.

44 Mardi Wilson, "Understanding Refusals, Using Coercion: Young Men's Understanding and Use of Normalized Sexualized Violence within

Heterosex," *Journal of Sex Research* 60, no. 8 (2023): 1168–1180, https://www.tandfonline.com/doi/full/10.1080/00224499.2022.2086676.

45 Natalie B. Compton, "It Took Me 12 Years to Realize I'd Been Raped," The Lily, April 23, 2021, https://www.thelily.com/it-took-me-12-years-to-realize-id-been-raped-promising-young-woman-triggered-that-breakthrough/.

46 Samantha Keene, "How We Can Help Dismantle Rape Culture," *Newsroom*, March 9, 2023, https://www.newsroom.co.nz/rape-culture-rough-sex-and-rape-trials.

47 Marian David, "The Correspondence Theory of Truth," *The Stanford Encyclopedia of Philosophy*, ed. Edward N. Zalta (Summer 2022 edition), https://plato.stanford.edu/archives/sum2022/entries/truth-correspondence/.

48 James O. Young, "The Coherence Theory of Truth," *The Stanford Encyclopedia of Philosophy*, ed. Edward N. Zalta (Fall 2018 edition), https://plato.stanford.edu/archives/fall2018/entries/truth-coherence/.

49 Catherine Legg and Christopher Hookway, "Pragmatism," *The Stanford Encyclopedia of Philosophy*, ed. Edward N. Zalta (Summer 2021 edition), https://plato.stanford.edu/archives/sum2021/entries/pragmatism/.

50 For an expanded discussion, see Chapter 2 of Robert Jensen, *Arguing for Our Lives: A User's Guide to Constructive Dialog* (San Francisco: City Lights, 2013).

51 Committee on the Use of Race, Ethnicity, and Ancestry as Population Descriptors in Genomics Research, *Using Population Descriptors in Genetics and Genomics Research: A New Framework for an Evolving Field* (National Academies of Sciences, Engineering, and Medicine: 2023), https://nap.nationalacademies.org/catalog/26902/using-population-descriptors-in-genetics-and-genomics-research-a-new.

52 For a more detailed account, see "Sex and Gender" in *The End of Patriarchy*, 19–34.

53 Naomi Oreskes, *Why Trust Science?* (Princeton, NJ: Princeton University Press, 2019).

54 Robert Jensen, *The Restless and Relentless Mind of Wes Jackson: Searching for Sustainability* (Lawrence: University Press of Kansas, 2021), 77–80; Bill Vitek and Wes Jackson, eds., *The Virtues of Ignorance: Complexity,*

Sustainability, and the Limits of Knowledge (Lexington: University Press of Kentucky, 2008).

55   "Intelligent Design: Is It Scientific?" University of California, Berkeley, https://undsci.berkeley.edu/intelligent-design-is-it-scientific/.

56   I add the term "premodern" in recognition that the term "indigenous" is applied to varying groups in inconsistent fashion. See Manvir Singh, "It's Time to Rethink the Idea of the 'Indigenous,'" *The New Yorker*, February 20, 2023, https://www.newyorker.com/magazine/2023/02/27/its-time-to-rethink-the-idea-of-the-indigenous.

57   Saima May Sidik, "Weaving the Lore of the Land into the Scientific Method," *Nature* 60, no. 13 (2022): 285–287, https://www.nature.com/articles/d41586-022-00029-2.

58   Angela Saini, *Superior: The Return of Race Science* (Boston: Beacon Press, 2019); Angela Saini, *Inferior: How Science Got Women Wrong—and the New Research That's Rewriting the Story* (Boston: Beacon Press, 2017).

59   Patrick Nunn, "Memories within Myth," Aeon, April 6, 2023, https://aeon.co/essays/the-stories-of-oral-societies-arent-myths-theyre-records.

60   Amy S. Groesbeck et al., "Ancient Clam Gardens Increased Shellfish Production: Adaptive Strategies from the Past Can Inform Food Security Today," *PLOS One*, March 11, 2014, https://journals.plos.org/plosone/article?id=10.1371/journal.pone.0091235.

61   George Nicholas, "It's Taken Thousands of Years, but Western Science Is Finally Catching Up to Traditional Knowledge," The Conversation, February 14, 2018, https://theconversation.com/its-taken-thousands-of-years-but-western-science-is-finally-catching-up-to-traditional-knowledge-90291.

62   Robin Wall Kimmerer, "Weaving Traditional Ecological Knowledge into Biological Education: A Call to Action," *BioScience* 52, no. 5 (2002): 432–438, https://academic.oup.com/bioscience/article/52/5/432/236145.

63   Ngozi Unuigbe, "What Can We Learn from Indigenous Ecological Knowledge?" *The Ecological Citizen* 6, no. 2 (2023), https://www.ecologicalcitizen.net/article.php?t=what-can-we-learn-indigenous-ecological-knowledge.

64   Gary Smith, "How Shoddy Data Becomes Sensational Research," *Chronicle of Higher Education*, June 6, 2023, https://www.chronicle.com/article/how-shoddy-data-becomes-sensational-research.

65   Clifford D. Conner, *The Tragedy of American Science: From Truman to Trump* (Chicago: Haymarket Books, 2020).

66   John P. A. Ioannidis, "Science Funding Is Broken," *Scientific American*, October 1, 2018, https://www.scientificamerican.com/article/science-funding-is-broken/.

67   Carolyn Merchant, "Environmentalism: From the Control of Nature to Partnerships" (Bernard Moses Memorial Lecture, University of California, Berkeley, May 4, 2010), https://nature.berkeley.edu/departments/espm/env-hist/Moses.pdf. See also Carolyn Merchant, *The Death of Nature: Women, Ecology and the Scientific Revolution* (San Francisco: Harper & Row, 1980).

68   Emmet Asher-Perrin, "Spock and the Myth of 'Emotion Versus Logic,'" Tor.com, September 17, 2019, https://www.tor.com/2019/09/17/spock-and-the-myth-of-emotion-versus-logic/.

69   That distinction is so routinely rejected in the sciences that a biologist titled a section of his book on human behavior "The Obligatory Declaration of the Falseness of the Dichotomy Between Cognition and Emotion." Robert M. Sapolsky, *Behave: The Biology of Humans at Our Best and Our Worst* (New York: Penguin Press, 2017), 54.

70   Robert H. Shmerling, "Right Brain/Left Brain, Right?" Harvard Health Publishing, March 24, 2022, https://www.health.harvard.edu/blog/right-brainleft-brain-right-2017082512222.

71   Sarah Lucia Hoagland, *Lesbian Ethics: Toward New Value* (Palo Alto, CA: Institute of Lesbian Studies, 1988), 186.

72   Naomi Scheman, "Anger and the Politics of Naming," in eds. Sally McConnell-Ginet, Ruth Borker, and Nelly Furman, *Women and Language in Literature and Society* (New York: Praeger, 1980), 177–178.

73   For a comprehensive account of these issues, see Judith Lewis Herman, *Trauma and Recovery* (New York: Basic Books, 1992) and Judith L. Herman, *Truth and Repair: How Trauma Survivors Envision Justice* (New York: Basic Books, 2023).

74   Vinod Goel, *Reason and Less: Pursuing Food, Sex, and Politics* (Cambridge, MA: MIT Press, 2022), 4.

75 Dacher Keltner and Paul Ekman, "The Science of 'Inside Out,'" *New York Times*, July 3, 2015, https://www.nytimes.com/2015/07/05/opinion/sunday/the-science-of-inside-out.html.

76 Daniel Kahneman, *Thinking Fast and Slow* (New York: Farrar, Straus and Giroux, 2013).

77 Steve Forbes, "Nobel Prize Winner Daniel Kahneman: Lessons from Hitler's SS and the Danger in Trusting Your Gut," *Forbes*, January 24, 2013, https://www.forbes.com/sites/steveforbes/2013/01/24/nobel-prize-winner-daniel-kahneman-lessons-from-hitlers-ss-and-the-danger-in-trusting-your-gut/?sh=35194fd9156e.

78 "Word of the Year 2016," Oxford Languages, https://languages.oup.com/word-of-the-year/2016/.

79 Hrishikesh Joshi, *Why It's OK to Speak Your Mind* (Abingdon, UK: Routledge, 2021), 3.

80 Hrishikesh Joshi, "Dare to Speak Your Mind and Together We Flourish," Psyche, June 7, 2021, https://psyche.co/ideas/dare-to-speak-your-mind-and-together-we-flourish.

81 Hugo Mercier and Dan Sperber, *The Enigma of Reason* (Cambridge, MA: Harvard University Press, 2017), 317.

CHAPTER 3:
STEPPING BACK: SPEAKING

82 This is a more accurate way to make the point than Stanley Fish did in his book *There's No Such Thing as Free Speech, and It's a Good Thing, Too* (New York: Oxford University Press, 1994).

83 Nadine Strossen, "Free Expression: An Endangered Species on Campus?" (Shorenstein Center on Media, Politics and Public Policy, Harvard Kennedy School, November 5, 2015), https://shorensteincenter.org/nadine-strossen-free-expression-an-endangered-species-on-campus-transcript/.

84 Zachary S. Price, "Our Imperiled Absolutist First Amendment," *University of Pennsylvania Journal of Constitutional Law* 20 (2018): 818.

85 Lynn Levine Greenky, *When Freedom Speaks: The Boundaries and the Boundlessness of Our First Amendment Right* (Waltham, MA: Brandeis University Press, 2022), 14.

86   Ian Tattersall, *Masters of the Planet: The Search for Our Human Origins* (New York: Palgrave Macmillan, 2012), xiv.

87   Absurd, perhaps, but routinely asserted by people in advertising. A professor I knew in a university advertising department once told me that any specific legal restrictions on advertising were inappropriate because "advertising is just information." He was ignoring the fact that advertisers spend billions of dollars a year not to provide consumers with accurate information but to undermine their ability to evaluate information in purchasing decisions.

88   John Stuart Mill, *On Liberty*, ed. Elizabeth Rapaport (Indianapolis: Hackett Publishing Co., 1978), 34. (Originally published 1859.)

89   *Schenck v. United States*, 249 U.S. 47 (1919).

90   *Brandenburg v. Ohio*, 395 U.S. 444 (1969).

91   "Sexual Harassment," US Equal Employment Opportunity Commission, https://www.eeoc.gov/sexual-harassment.

92   "Policy Guidance on Current Issues of Sexual Harassment," US Equal Employment Opportunity Commission, https://www.eeoc.gov/laws/guidance/policy-guidance-current-issues-sexual-harassment.

93   "Sexual Harassment Guidance: Harassment of Students by School Employees, Other Students, or Third Parties," US Department of Education Office for Civil Rights, Federal Register, 62:49 (March 13, 1997), https://www.govinfo.gov/content/pkg/FR-1997-03-13/html/97-6373.htm.

94   David Buss, "Sexual Violence Laws: Policy Implications of Psychological Sex Differences," *Evolution and Human Behavior* 44, no. 3 (2023): 278–283, https://www.sciencedirect.com/science/article/abs/pii/S109051382300003X?via%3Dihub.

95   "Race/Color Discrimination," US Equal Employment Opportunity Commission, https://www.eeoc.gov/racecolor-discrimination.

CHAPTER 4:
DEFINING RACISM: INDIVIDUAL BIGOTRY AND BEYOND

96   This phrase is credited to Peggy McIntosh, "White Privilege: Unpacking the Invisible Knapsack," *Peace and Freedom Magazine*, July/

August 1989, 10–12, https://nationalseedproject.org/Key-SEED-Texts/white-privilege-unpacking-the-invisible-knapsack.

97 Articles are archived at https://robertwjensen.org/topics/race/.

98 Robert Jensen, *The Heart of Whiteness: Confronting Race, Racism and White Privilege* (San Francisco: City Lights Books, 2005).

99 *James Baldwin: Collected Essays* (New York: Library of America, 1998).

100 Andre Rhoden-Paul, "Ngozi Fulani: Lady Susan Hussey's Race Comments Were Abuse, Says Charity Boss," BBC, December 1, 2022, https://www.bbc.com/news/uk-63819482.

101 Sean Coughlan, "Lady Susan Hussey Quits over Remarks to Charity Boss Ngozi Fulani," BBC, December 1, 2022, https://www.bbc.com/news/uk-63810468.

102 Noel Ignatiev, *How the Irish Became White* (New York: Routledge, 1995).

103 Cristina Beltrán, "To Understand Trump's Support, We Must Think in Terms of Multiracial Whiteness," *Washington Post*, January 15, 2021, https://www.washingtonpost.com/opinions/2021/01/15/understand-trumps-support-we-must-think-terms-multiracial-whiteness/.

104 Cecilia Márquez, "The Long and Violent History of Anti-Black Racism in the Latino Community," *New York Times*, May 12, 2023, https://www.nytimes.com/2023/05/12/opinion/allen-texas-shooting.html; Tanya Katerí Hernández, *Racial Innocence: Unmasking Latino Anti-Black Bias and the Struggle for Equality* (Boston: Beacon, 2022).

105 Paul Buter, "Are the Men Kyle Rittenhouse Killed Victims? Not According to the Judge," *Washington Post*, October 29, 2021, https://www.washingtonpost.com/opinions/2021/10/29/are-men-kyle-rittenhouse-killed-victims-not-according-judge/.

106 Yarimar Bonilla, "Enrique Tarrio and the Curious Case of the Latino White Supremacist," *New York Times*, August 19, 2023, https://www.nytimes.com/2023/08/19/opinion/enrique-tarrio-proud-boys-latinos-racism.html. Tarrio was convicted of seditious conspiracy in the January 6 case and sentenced to twenty-two years in prison.

107 Lawrence Blum, *"I'm Not a Racist, But…": The Moral Quandary of Race* (Ithaca, NY: Cornell University Press, 2002).

108   Robert Jensen, "I Know I'm a Racist but ...: The Language and Rhetoric of Race," *New Impact* magazine, January 2002, http://www.raceandhistory.com/ historicalviews/2002/1605.htm.

109   Travis J. Bristol, Matthew Shirrell, and Tolani Britton, "How Does Student-Teacher Matching Affect Suspensions for Students of Color?" Brookings Institution, October 11, 2021, https://www.brookings.edu/ blog/brown-center-chalkboard/2021/10/11/how-does-student-teacher-matching-affect-suspensions-for-students-of-color/.

110   Gwen Dewar, "Not Actually Angry: Black Children and Boys More Frequently Misjudged," Parenting Science, August 20, 2020, https://parentingscience.com/biases-against-kids-misreading-anger/.

111   National Center for Education Statistics, "Race and Ethnicity of Public School Teachers and Their Students," US Department of Education, September 2020, https://nces.ed.gov/pubs2020/2020103/index.asp.

112   Madeline Will, "Teachers Are as Racially Biased as Everybody Else, Study Shows," *Education Week*, June 9, 2020, https://www.edweek.org/ teaching-learning/teachers-are-as-racially-biased-as-everybody-else-study-shows/2020/06.

113   Tara García Mathewson, "New Data: Even within the Same District Some Wealthy Schools Get Millions More Than Poor Ones," The Hechinger Report, October 31, 2020, https://hechingerreport.org/ new-data-even-within-the-same-district-some-wealthy-schools-get-millions-more-than-poor-ones/.

114   Neil Bhutta et al., "Disparities in Wealth by Race and Ethnicity in the 2019 Survey of Consumer Finances," Federal Reserve System, FEDS Notes, September 28, 2020, https://www.federalreserve.gov/econres/ notes/feds-notes/disparities-in-wealth-by-race-and-ethnicity-in-the-2019-survey-of-consumer-finances-20200928.html.

115   Tracy Hadden Loh, Christopher Coes, and Becca Buthe, "Separate and Unequal: Persistent Residential Segregation Is Sustaining Racial and Economic Injustice in the U.S.," Brookings Institution, December 16, 2020, https://www.brookings.edu/articles/trend-1-separate-and-unequal-neighborhoods-are-sustaining-racial-and-economic-injustice-in-the-us/.

116   For an example, see "What Two Starkly Different Philly-Area High Schools Tell Us about How Pa. Funds Education," Schooled

podcast, WHYY, June 14, 2023, https://whyy.org/episodes/
philadelphia-high-school-funding-pennsylvania-schooled-season-6-
episode-1-penn-wood-lower-merion/.

117 Alana Semuels, "Good School, Rich School; Bad School, Poor School,"
The Atlantic, August 25, 2016, https://www.theatlantic.com/business/
archive/2016/08/property-taxes-and-unequal-schools/497333/.

118 Lynne Peeples, "What the Data Say about Police Brutality and Racial
Bias—and Which Reforms Might Work," *Nature*, May 26, 2021,
https://www.nature.com/articles/d41586-020-01846-z.

119 Frank Edwards, Hedwig Lee, and Michael Esposito, "Risk of Being Killed by
Police Use of Force in the United States by Age, Race-Ethnicity, and Sex,"
PNAS, August 5, 2019, https://www.pnas.org/doi/10.1073/pnas.1821204116.

120 Ashley Nellis, "The Color of Justice: Racial and Ethnic Disparity
in State Prisons," The Sentencing Project, October 13, 2021,
https://www.sentencingproject.org/reports/the-color-of-justice-racial-and-
ethnic-disparity-in-state-prisons-the-sentencing-project/.

121 Jeffrey Bellin, *Mass Incarceration Nation: How the United States Became
Addicted to Prisons and Jails and How It Can Recover* (Cambridge, UK:
Cambridge University Press, 2022).

122 World Prison Brief, https://www.prisonstudies.org/world-prison-brief-data.

123 Zack Beauchamp, "What the Police Really Believe," Vox, July 7,
2020, https://www.vox.com/policy-and-politics/2020/7/7/21293259/
police-racism-violence-ideology-george-floyd.

124 Joseph Goldstein and Ashley Southall, "'I Got Tired of Hunting Black and
Hispanic People,'" *New York Times*, December 6, 2019, https://www.nytimes.
com/2019/12/06/nyregion/nyc-police-subway-racial-profiling.html.

125 Clyde McGrady, "Tyre Nichols Beating Opens a Complex Conversation on
Race and Policing," *New York Times*, January 28, 2023, https://www.nytimes.
com/2023/01/28/us/police-tyre-nichols-beating-race.html.

126 Sam Mitrani, "The Police Were Created to Control Working Class and
Poor People, Not 'Serve and Protect,'" *In These Times*, January 6, 2015,
https://inthesetimes.com/article/police-and-poor-people.

127 Diana R. Gordon, *Return of the Dangerous Classes: Drug Prohibition and
Policy Politics* (New York: W.W. Norton, 1994).

128   Ames Grawert and Terry-Ann Craigie, "Mass Incarceration Has Been a Driving Force of Economic Inequality," Brennan Center for Justice, November 4, 2020, https://www.brennancenter.org/our-work/analysis-opinion/mass-incarceration-has-been-driving-force-economic-inequality.

129   Mackenzie Buday and Ashley Nellis, "Private Prisons in the United States," The Sentencing Project, August 23, 2022, https://www.sentencingproject.org/reports/private-prisons-in-the-united-states/.

130   Joshua Page, *The Toughest Beat: Politics, Punishment, and the Prison Officers Union in California* (Oxford: Oxford University Press, 2011).

131   For an extensive collection of studies that demonstrate this, see Radley Balko, "There's Overwhelming Evidence That the Criminal Justice System Is Racist. Here's the Proof," *Washington Post*, June 10, 2020, https://www.washingtonpost.com/graphics/2020/opinions/systemic-racism-police-evidence-criminal-justice-system/.

132   Joe Soss and Vesla Weaver, "Police Are Our Government: Politics, Political Science, and the Policing of Race-Class Subjugated Communities," *Annual Review of Political Science* 20 (2017): 565–591, https://www.annualreviews.org/doi/abs/10.1146/annurev-polisci-060415-093825.

133   Jeffrey Reiman and Paul Leighton, *The Rich Get Richer and the Poor Get Prison: Thinking Critically about Class and Criminal Justice*, 12th ed. (New York: Routledge, 2020).

134   Jill Lepore, "The Invention of the Police," *The New Yorker*, July 13, 2020, https://www.newyorker.com/magazine/2020/07/20/the-invention-of-the-police.

135   David Brooks, "You Are Not Who You Think You Are," *New York Times*, September 2, 2021, https://www.nytimes.com/2021/09/02/opinion/brain-reality-imagination.html.

136   Michael Powell, "M.I.T.'s Choice of Lecturer Ignited Criticism. So Did Its Decision to Cancel," *New York Times*, October 20, 2021, https://www.nytimes.com/2021/10/20/us/dorian-abbot-mit.html.

137   Phoebe Cohen, "Becoming Clickbait for Speaking Out," Inside Higher Ed, November 8, 2021, https://www.insidehighered.com/views/2021/11/08/professor-targeted-views-dorian-abbot-incident-opinion.

138   Tema Okun, "White Supremacy Culture," 1999, https://www.whitesupremacyculture.info/uploads/4/3/5/7/43579015/okun_-

_white_sup_culture_2020.pdf and https://www.whitesupremacyculture.info/characteristics.html.

139   Robert Jensen, *Writing Dissent: Taking Radical Ideas from the Margins to the Mainstream* (New York: Peter Lang, 2001); Robert Jensen, "Beyond Advocacy v. Objective Journalism," Mediabite, July 5, 2007, https://mediabite.org/2007/07/05/beyond-advocacy-v-objective-journalism/.

140   That does happen. See Tabia Lee, "A Black DEI Director Canceled by DEI," *Compact*, March 31, 2023, https://compactmag.com/article/a-black-dei-director-canceled-by-dei.

141   Ryan Grim, "Tema Okun on Her Mythical Paper on White Supremacy," The Intercept, February 3, 2023, https://theintercept.com/2023/02/03/deconstructed-tema-okun-white-supremacy/.

142   Tema Okun, "White Supremacy Culture – Still Here," 2021, https://drive.google.com/file/d/1XR_7M_9qa64zZoo_JyFVTAjmjVU-uSz8/view.

143   Conor Friedersdorf, "How to Make Diversity Trainings Better," *The Atlantic*, January 23, 2023, https://www.theatlantic.com/newsletters/archive/2023/01/how-to-make-diversity-trainings-better/672815/; Lily Zheng, "The Failure of the DEI-Industrial Complex," *Harvard Business Review*, December 1, 2022, https://hbr.org/2022/12/the-failure-of-the-dei-industrial-complex; Bridget Read, "Doing the Work at Work: What are Companies Desperate for Diversity Consultants Actually Buying?" The Cut/*New York Magazine*, May 26, 2021, https://www.thecut.com/article/diversity-equity-inclusion-industrial-companies.html.

144   Betsy Levy Paluck, "Does Diversity Training Work? We Don't Know—and Here Is Why," *Washington Post*, December 12, 2022, https://www.washingtonpost.com/opinions/2022/12/12/diversity-training-effectiveness-psychologist/; Elizabeth Levy Paluck et al., "Prejudice Reduction: Progress and Challenges," *Annual Review of Psychology* 72 (2021): 533–560, https://www.annualreviews.org/doi/10.1146/annurev-psych-071620-030619.

145   For an example of such self-reflection, see Musa al-Gharbi, "Diversity-Related Training: What Is it Good For?" Heterodox: The Blog, September 16, 2020, https://heterodoxacademy.org/blog/diversity-related-training-what-is-it-good-for/.

146 Coleman Hughes and Jamelle Bouie, "Does Color Blindness Perpetuate Racism?" Open to Debate and TED, July 2023, https://www.ted.com/talks/ coleman_hughes_and_jamelle_bouie does_color_blindness_perpetuatc_ racism.

147 These paragraphs reflect insights offered by Pat Youngblood in private conversation.

148 Tyler Austin Harper, "I'm a Black Professor. You Don't Need to Bring That Up," *The Atlantic*, August 14, 2023, https://www.theatlantic.com/ ideas/archive/2023/08/anti-racist-color-blindness-dei-programs/674996/.

149 Benjamin Wallace-Wells, "How a Conservative Activist Invented the Conflict over Critical Race Theory," *The New Yorker*, June 18, 2021, https://www.newyorker.com/news/annals-of-inquiry/how-a-conservative- activist-invented-the-conflict-over-critical-race-theory.

150 CS/HB 7: Individual Freedom, Florida Senate, 2022, https://www.flsenate.gov/ Session/Bill/2022/7.

151 Stacie Brensilver Berman, Robert Cohen, and Ryan Mills, "Why CRT Belongs in the Classroom, and How to Do It Right," History News Network, January 22, 2023, https://historynewsnetwork.org/article/184803.

CHAPTER 6:
DEFINING ECOLOGICAL SUSTAINABILITY: FEWER AND LESS

152 Wendell Berry, "Sabbaths 2007, VI," in *Leavings: Poems* (Berkeley, CA: Counterpoint, 2010), 91–93.

153 Noam Chomsky, "The Responsibility of Intellectuals," *New York Review of Books*, February 23, 1967, https://www.nybooks.com/articles/1967/02/23/ a-special-supplement-the-responsibility-of-intelle/.

154 Mathis Wackernagel and William E. Rees, *Our Ecological Footprint: Reducing Human Impact on the Earth* (Gabriola Island, BC: New Society Publishers, 1996).

155 William R. Catton Jr., *Overshoot: The Ecological Basis of Revolutionary Change* (Urbana: University of Illinois Press, 1980).

156 Robert Jensen, "The Old Future's Gone: Progressive Strategy amid Cascading Crises" (lecture, Interfaith Summer Institute for Justice, Peace

and Social Movements, Simon Fraser University, Vancouver, BC, August 11, 2008), https://www.countercurrents.org/jensen200808.htm.

157 Robert Jensen, "Nature Bats Last: Notes on Revolution and Resistance, Revelation and Redemption" (lecture, Veterans for Peace national conference, Portland, OR, August 4, 2011), https://truthout.org/articles/nature-bats-last-notes-on-revolution-and-resistance-revelation-and-redemption/.

158 Robert Jensen, "We Are All Apocalyptic Now: Moral Responsibilities in Crisis Times" (lecture, First Unitarian Universalist Church Public Affairs Forum, Austin, TX, February 24, 2013), www.youtube.com/watch?v=aqgigYmr86Y. I first used the phrase in print in "Rationally Speaking, We Are All Apocalyptic Now," Truthout, February 8, 2013, https://truthout.org/articles/rationally-speaking-we-are-all-apocalyptic-now/. That was followed by a long pamphlet: *We Are All Apocalyptic Now: On the Responsibilities of Teaching, Preaching, Reporting, Writing, and Speaking Out* (self-pub., CreateSpace, 2013).

159 Wes Jackson and Robert Jensen, *An Inconvenient Apocalypse: Environmental Collapse, Climate Crisis, and the Fate of Humanity* (South Bend, IN: University of Notre Dame Press, 2022).

160 Jackson and Jensen, *An Inconvenient Apocalypse*, Chapter 2.

161 This is updated and expanded from Robert Jensen, *Arguing for Our Lives: A User's Guide to Constructive Dialog* (San Francisco: City Lights, 2013), 106–109.

162 Surplus-and-hierarchy predate agriculture only in a few resource-rich places. See Heather Pringle, "The Ancient Roots of the 1%," *Science* 344, no. 6186 (2014): 822–25, www.science.org/lookup/doi/10.1126/science.344.6186.822

163 David Graeber and David Wengrow, *The Dawn of Everything: A New History of Humanity* (New York: Farrar, Straus and Giroux, 2021).

164 "Old Future," track 7 on John Gorka, *Old Futures Gone*, Red House Records, 2003, CD.

165 Paul Krugman, "The Promise and Peril of Biden's Climate Policy," *New York Times*, March 2, 2023, https://www.nytimes.com/2023/03/02/opinion/biden-climate-policy.html.

166 Ronald Wright, *A Short History of Progress* (New York: Carroll & Graf Publishers, 2005).

167 Ronald Wright, "Can We Still Dodge the Progress Trap?" The Tyee, September 20, 2019, https://thetyee.ca/Analysis/2019/09/20/ Ronald-Wright-Can-We-Dodge-Progress-Trap/.

168 Vaclav Smil, "Energy in the Twentieth Century: Resources, Conversions, Costs, Uses, and Consequences," *Annual Review of Energy and the Environment* 25 (2000): 23, https://www.annualreviews.org/doi/10.1146/ annurev.energy.25.1.21.

169 Vaclav Smil, "World History and Energy," in *Encyclopedia of Energy*, ed. Cutler J. Cleveland, Volume 6 (Amsterdam Netherlands: Elsevier Academic Press, 2004), 557.

170 "UN Report: Nature's Dangerous Decline 'Unprecedented'; Species Extinction Rates 'Accelerating,'" Sustainable Development Goals, May 6, 2019, https://www.un.org/sustainabledevelopment/blog/2019/05/ nature-decline-unprecedented-report/.

171 Catrin Einhorn, "A 'Crossroads' for Humanity: Earth's Biodiversity Is Still Collapsing," *New York Times*, September 15, 2020, https://www.nytimes.com/ 2020/09/15/climate/biodiversity-united-nations-report.html.

172 "Global Biodiversity Outlook 5," Secretariat of the Convention on Biological Diversity, 2020, https://www.cbd.int/gbo/gbo5/publication/ gbo-5-en.pdf.

173 Andrew J. Plumptre et al., "Where Might We Find Ecologically Intact Communities?" *Frontiers in Forests and Global Change* 4 (April 2021), https://www.frontiersin.org/articles/10.3389/ffgc.2021.626635/full. One definition of intactness is "an ecological community having the complete complement of species known or expected to occur in a particular site or ecosystem, relative to a regionally appropriate historical benchmark, which will often correspond to pre-industrial times."

174 Stewart Patrick, "To Prevent the Collapse of Biodiversity, the World Needs a New Planetary Politics," Carnegie Endowment for International Peace, November 28, 2022, https://carnegieendowment.org/2022/11/28/ to-prevent-collapse-of-biodiversity-world-needs-new-planetary-politics- pub-88473.

175 "The Global Risks Report 2023," World Economic Forum, January 11, 2023, https://www3.weforum.org/docs/WEF_Global_Risks_Report_2023.pdf.

176 "World Population to Reach 8 Billion this Year, as Growth Rate Slows," UN News, July 11, 2022, https://news.un.org/en/story/2022/07/1122272.

177 Nils Petter Gleditsch, "This Time Is Different! Or Is It? NeoMalthusians and Environmental Optimists in the Age of Climate Change," *Journal of Peace Research* 58, no. 1 (2021): 177–185, https://journals.sagepub.com/doi/full/10.1177/0022343320969785.

178 For an excellent explanation of why these issues shouldn't be ignored, see John Mirisch, "I Know You're Malthusian, But What Am I?" Steady State Herald, April 20, 2023, https://steadystate.org/i-know-youre-malthusian-but-what-am-i/.

179 Sam Knights, "The Climate Movement Must Be Ready To Challenge Rising Right-Wing Environmentalism," Jacobin, November 16, 2020, https://jacobin.com/2020/11/climate-change-right-wing-environmentalism-alt-right-eco-fascism.

180 Ruxandra Guidi, "Eco-Fascism, Uncovered," *Sierra*, December 27, 2022, https://www.sierraclub.org/sierra/4-november-december/feature/eco-fascism-uncovered-el-paso-texas.

181 One such group combining progressive politics and ecological awareness is Population Balance, https://www.populationbalance.org/. See Nandita Bajaj and Kirsten Stade, "Challenging Pronatalism Is Key to Advancing Reproductive Rights and a Sustainable Population," *Journal of Population and Sustainability* 7, no. 21 (2023): 39–69, https://www.whp-journals.co.uk/JPS/article/view/819.

182 David Marchese, "This Eminent Scientist Says Climate Activists Need to Get Real," *New York Times Magazine*, April 22, 2022, https://www.nytimes.com/interactive/2022/04/25/magazine/vaclav-smil-interview.html.

183 Jem Bendell, "Beyond Fed Up: Six Hard Trends that Lead to Food System Breakdown," Institute for Leadership and Sustainability, Occasional Papers 10 (2023), https://insight.cumbria.ac.uk/id/eprint/6927/.

184 Smil, "Energy in the Twentieth Century," 35–36.

185 Vaclav Smil, *Enriching the Earth: Fritz Haber, Carl Bosch, and the Transformation of World Food Production* (Cambridge, MA: MIT Press, 2000).

186   Hannah Ritchie, "How Many People Does Synthetic Fertilizer Feed?"
       Our World in Data, November 7, 2017, https://ourworldindata.org/
       how-many-people-does-synthetic-fertilizer-feed.

187   Mark Buchanan, "Deep Warming: Even If We 'Solve' Global Warming,
       We Face an Older, Slower Problem," Aeon, June 8, 2023, https://aeon.co/
       essays/theres-a-deeper-problem-hiding-beneath-global-warming.

188   For an example, see Jared Strong, "Town's Drinking Water
       Contamination Returns after Testing Ends," Iowa Capital Dispatch,
       January 17, 2023, https://iowacapitaldispatch.com/2023/01/17/
       towns-drinking-water-contamination-returns-after-testing-ends/.

189   Elizabeth Kolbert, "Phosphorus Saved Our Way of Life—and
       Now Threatens to End It," *The New Yorker*, February 27,
       2023, https://www.newyorker.com/magazine/2023/03/06/
       phosphorus-saved-our-way-of-life-and-now-threatens-to-end-it.

190   David Montgomery, *Dirt: The Erosion of Civilizations*, 2nd ed. (Berkeley:
       University of California Press, 2012), xii.

191   Stan Rowe, "The Living Earth and Its Ethical Priority," *The Trumpeter* 19,
       no. 2 (2003), https://emmind.net/openpapers_repos/Earth_Fields-Gaia/
       Various/Gaia/2003_The_Living_Earth_and_Its_Ethical_Priority.pdf.

192   Michael Huesemann and Joyce Huesemann, *Techno-Fix: Why
       Technology Won't Save Us or the Environment* (Gabriola Island, BC:
       New Society, 2011); Tim Healy, "The Unanticipated Consequences
       of Technology," Markkula Center for Applied Ethics, April 6, 2005,
       https://www.scu.edu/ethics/focus-areas/technology-ethics/resources/
       the-unanticipated-consequences-of-technology/.

193   Evgeny Morozov, *Save Everything, Click Here: The Folly of Technological
       Solutionism* (New York: PublicAffairs, 2013), 6.

194   Mark Lynas, *The God Species: Saving the Planet in the Age of Humans*
       (Washington, DC: National Geographic Society, 2011), 10.

195   Replanet, https://www.replanet.ngo/.

196   John Asafu-Adjaye et al., "An Ecomodernist Manifesto," 2015,
       http://www.ecomodernism.org/manifesto-english/.

197   Stewart Brand, "Purpose," *Whole Earth Catalog* (n.p., 1968),
       https://monoskop.org/images/0/09/Brand_Stewart_Whole_Earth_
       Catalog_Fall_1968.pdf.

198 Stewart Brand, *Whole Earth Discipline: An Ecopragmatist Manifesto* (New York: Viking Adult, 2009), 1.

199 Stewart Brand, "Reviving Extinct Species," The Long Now Foundation, May 21, 2013, https://longnow.org/seminars/02013/may/21/reviving-extinct-species/.

200 William E. Rees, "Overshoot: Cognitive Obsolescence and the Population Conundrum," *Population and Sustainability* 7, no. 1 (2023): 15, https://www.whp-journals.co.uk/JPS/article/view/855.

201 James Howard Kunstler, *Too Much Magic: Wishful Thinking, Technology, and the Fate of the Nation* (New York: Atlantic Monthly Press, 2012), 7.

202 Rex Tillerson, "The New North American Energy Paradigm: Reshaping the Future," Council on Foreign Relations, June 27, 2012, https://www.cfr.org/event/new-north-american-energy-paradigm-reshaping-future.

203 John McMurtry, *The Cancer Stage of Capitalism: From Crisis to Cure*, 2nd ed. (London: Pluto Press, 2013).

204 Vaclav Smil, *How the World Really Works: The Science Behind How We Got Here and Where We're Going* (New York: Viking, 2022); Michael J. Kelly, "Feasibility for Achieving a Net Zero Economy for the U.S. by 2050," Climate Etc., March 4, 2023, https://judithcurry.com/2023/03/04/feasibility-for-chieving-a-net-zero-economy-for-the-u-s-in-2050/; Andrew Nikiforuk, "The Rising Chorus of Renewable Energy Skeptics," The Tyee, April 7, 2023, https://thetyee.ca/Analysis/2023/04/07/Rising-Chorus-Renewable-Energy-Skeptics/.

205 Alexandre Antonelli, "Indigenous Knowledge Is Key to Sustainable Food Systems," *Nature* 613 (January 12, 2023): 239-242, https://www.nature.com/articles/d41586-023-00021-4.

206 Kennon Sheldon, "The Three Reasons Why It's Good for You To Believe in Free Will," Psyche, June 15, 2023, https://psyche.co/ideas/the-three-reasons-why-its-good-for-you-to-believe-in-free-will; Stephen Cave, "There's No Such Thing as Free Will, but We're Better Off Believing in It Anyway," *The Atlantic*, June 2016, https://www.theatlantic.com/magazine/archive/2016/06/theres-no-such-thing-as-free-will/480750/. See also, Robert M. Sapolsky, *Determined: A Science of Life without Free Will* (New York: Penguin Press, 2023).

207 See, for example, Chris Knight, "Wrong About (Almost) Everything," FocaalBlog/*Focaal: Journal of Global and Historical Anthropology*, December 22, 2021, https://www.focaalblog.com/2021/12/22/ chris-knight-wrong-about-almost-everything/.

208 Kwame Anthony Appiah, "Digging for Utopia," *New York Review of Books*, December 16, 2021, https://www.nybooks.com/articles/2021/12/16/ david-graeber-digging-for-utopia/.

209 Kwame Anthony Appiah, "The Roots of Inequality: An Exchange," *New York Review of Books*, January 13, 2022, https://www.nybooks.com/ articles/2022/01/13/the-roots-of-inequality-an-exchange/.

210 For a more in-depth argument, see Chapter 1 of *An Inconvenient Apocalypse*.

211 William E. Rees, "The Human Eco-Predicament: Overshoot and the Population Conundrum," *Vienna Yearbook of Population Research* 21 (2023): 1–19, https://www.austriaca.at/?arp=0x003dcfa1.

212 Larry Edwards and Stan Cox, "Cap and Adapt: A Failsafe Approach to the Climate Emergency," The Climate Mobilization, August 28, 2019, https://www.theclimatemobilization.org/blog/2019/08/28/ cap-and-adapt-a-failsafe-approach-to-the-climate-emergency/.

213 Stan Cox, *Any Way You Slice It: The Past, Present, and Future of Rationing* (New York: New Press, 2013).

214 Nina Lakhani, "Revealed: How US Transition to Electric Cars Threatens Environmental Havoc," *The Guardian*, January 24, 2023, https://www.theguardian.com/us-news/2023/jan/24/us-electric-vehicles-lithium-consequences-research; Siddharth Kara, *Cobalt Red: How the Blood of the Congo Powers Our Lives* (New York: St. Martin's Press, 2023).

215 Shannon Osaka, "Minerals Are Crucial for Electric Cars and Wind Turbines. Some Worry Whether We Have Enough," *Washington Post*, February 2, 2023, https://www.washingtonpost.com/climate-environment/2023/02/02/critical-minerals-run-out-shortage/; Aaron Steckelberg et al., "The Underbelly of Electric Vehicles," *Washington Post*, April 27, 2023, https://www.washingtonpost.com/world/interactive/2023/ electric-car-batteries-geography/.

216 Geoffrey Supran, Stefan Rahmstorf, and Naomi Oreskes, "Assessing ExxonMobil's Global Warming Projections," *Science* 379, no. 6628 (2023), https://www.science.org/doi/10.1126/science.abk0063.

217 Joshua Floyd et al., "Energy Descent as a Post-Carbon Transition Scenario: How 'Knowledge Humility' Reshapes Energy Futures for Post-Normal Times," *Futures* 122 (Sept. 2020), https://www.sciencedirect.com/science/article/abs/pii/S0016328720300550; Christopher Ketcham, "Green-Tinted Glasses: The Green Growth Delusion," Truthdig, April 4, 2023, https://www.truthdig.com/dig/green-tinted-glasses/; Patrick Moriarty and Damon Honnery, "The Limits of Renewable Energy," *AIMS Energy* 9, no. 4 (2021): 812–829, https://www.aimspress.com/article/doi/10.3934/energy.2021037.

218 "US Energy Facts Explained," US Energy Information Administration, https://www.eia.gov/energyexplained/us-energy-facts/.

CONCLUSION:
WHERE ARE WE GOING?

219 The book was published under Mill's name, though some scholars believe that his wife, Harriet Taylor Mill, should be credited as a coauthor. Christoph Schmidt-Petri, Michael Schefczyk, and Lilly Osburg, "Who Authored *On Liberty*? Stylometric Evidence on Harriet Taylor Mill's Contribution," *Utilitas* 34, no. 2 (2022): 120–138, https://www.cambridge.org/core/journals/utilitas/article/who-authored-on-liberty-stylometric-evidence-on-harriet-taylor-mills-contribution/1FA7F6104FDC4CE23146D71B26F740C6.

220 Mill, *On Liberty*, 50.

221 Mill, *On Liberty*, 34.

222 Duncan Bell, "John Stuart Mill on Colonies," *Political Theory* 38, no. 1 (2010): 37, https://journals.sagepub.com/doi/10.1177/0090591709348186.

223 Mill, *On Liberty*, 52.

224 Mill, *On Liberty*, 28.

225 Robert Jensen, "U.S. Just as Guilty of Committing Own Violent Acts," *Houston Chronicle*, September 14, 2001, A-33, https://robertwjensen.org/articles/u-s-just-as-guilty-of-committing-own-violent-acts/

226 Lee Nichols, "War of Words: UT Professor Gets Slammed by the UT President in *Houston Chronicle* for View on Attacks," *Austin Chronicle*, September 28, 2001, https://www.austinchronicle.com/news/2001-09-28/83161/.

227 "Costs of War," Watson Institute, Brown University, https://watson.brown.edu/costsofwar/.

228 Robert Jensen, "Some Basic Propositions about Sex, Gender, and Patriarchy," Dissident Voice, June 13, 2014, https://dissidentvoice.org/2014/06/some-basic-propositions-about-sex-gender-and-patriarchy/.

229 "A Note on Bob Jensen," Monkeywrench Books, 2014, https://us7.campaign-archive.com/?u=6cd8e997251fc0b0a88b19ea2&id=a48679cee3&e=1ca6c3321c.

230 For one example, see C. Kistler, "RATPAC-ATX : Regarding the Disruption of Robert Jensen," Redspark, March 12, 2017, https://www.redspark.nu/en/proletarian-feminism/ratpac-atx-regarding-the-disruption-of-robert-jensen/.

231 "Allow Women and Girls to Speak on Sex, Gender and Gender Identity Without Intimidation or Fear: UN Expert," quoting Reem Alsalem, Special Rapporteur on Violence against Women and Girls, UN Human Rights Office of the High Commissioner, May 22, 2023, https://www.ohchr.org/en/press-releases/2023/05/allow-women-and-girls-speak-sex-gender-and-gender-identity-without.

232 Haroon Siddique, "Maya Forstater Was Discriminated against over Gender-Critical Beliefs, Tribunal Rules," *The Guardian*, July 6, 2022, https://www.theguardian.com/society/2022/jul/06/maya-forstater-was-discriminated-against-over-gender-critical-beliefs-tribunal-rules.

233 Gina Davidson, "Feminist Speaker Julie Bindel 'Attacked by Transgender Person' at Edinburgh University after Talk," *The Scotsman*, June 6, 2019, https://www.scotsman.com/news/scottish-news/feminist-speaker-julie-bindel-attacked-by-transgender-person-at-edinburgh-university-after-talk-545841; Tom Slater, "'Punch a TERF': The Violent Misogyny of the Trans Movement," Spiked, July 10, 2023, https://www.spiked-online.com/2023/07/10/punch-a-terf-the-violent-misogyny-of-the-trans-movement/.

234 "What Is Homophobic, Biphobic and Transphobic Bullying?" Stonewall, https://www.stonewall.org.uk/what-homophobic-biphobic-and-transphobic-bullying.

235 Robert Jensen, "What Is Really Radical in Sex/Gender Politics?" Culturico, July 26, 2020, https://culturico.com/2020/07/26/what-is-really-radical-in-sex-gender-politics/.

236 Ralph Waldo Emerson, "Self-Reliance," in *Essays: First Series* (1841), https://archive.vcu.edu/english/engweb/transcendentalism/authors/emerson/essays/selfreliance.html.

237 Robert Jensen, *Plain Radical: Living, Loving, and Learning to Leave the Planet Gracefully* (Berkeley, CA: Counterpoint/Soft Skull, 2015).

238 Karl Marx, letter to Arnold Ruge, September 1843, http://www.marxists.org/archive/marx/works/1843/letters/43_09.htm.

239 Martin Luther King Jr., *Where Do We Go from Here: Chaos or Community?* (New York: Harper & Row, 1967).

240 Wes Jackson, *Hogs Are Up: Stories of the Land, with Digressions* (Lawrence: University Press of Kansas, 2021), 153.

Index

About the Author

Robert Jensen is Emeritus Professor in the School of Journalism and Media at the University of Texas at Austin and collaborates with the New Perennials Project at Middlebury College. He is co-author with Wes Jackson of *An Inconvenient Apocalypse: Environmental Collapse, Climate Crisis, and the Fate of Humanity* and the editor of *From the Ground Up: Conversations with Wes Jackson*, based on the interviews from "Podcast from the Prairie." Jensen is the author of 10 other books, including *The End of Patriarchy: Radical Feminism for Men*; *Plain Radical: Living, Loving, and Learning to Leave the Planet Gracefully*; and *The Heart of Whiteness: Confronting Race, Racism and White Privilege*.